Dick Anderson tells how ⟨...⟩ drove him to be a mission⟨...⟩ in Kenya and in the end ⟨...⟩ pioneering ventures over ⟨...⟩ ⟨...⟩ unreached peoples in Mozambique, Sudan, Chad, Madagascar, the Comoros, and Seychelles Islands in the Indian Ocean. He hides nothing of the risks, the privations faced, the impact on his wife and family, and the deep personal struggles he went through. This is a 'must read' for those who feel called to take the gospel to unreached peoples.

Rev Tom Houston

It has been a privilege to know Dick Anderson as my Christian brother, friend and mentor in missionary matters. Despite this relationship I felt sure there were depths of wisdom and experience hidden by his self-effacement. I am glad that he overcame this obstacle by making these valuable reminiscences available in print. His story is an enthralling account of the beginnings of Christian work in a number of African countries where I have personally witnessed the abiding fruit of his diligent labours.

No one reading this biography will remain unchallenged. It is a thrilling and gripping account of risks undertaken and dangers faced for the sake of the Gospel. Esteem for Africans and an understanding of their cultures were basic to the work attempted among them and will be instructive to anyone called to cross-cultural communication. Dick and his devoted wife Joan were driven by a passion for the conversion of Africans to Christ and the founding of churches. Underlying their zeal was the conviction that time is short, and that the test of such a work is not in buildings and institutions but in the vitality of the church ten years after all missionaries have departed.

This book will challenge those who build a comfort-zone around their chosen sphere of service, and those who insist on a conditional response to the great commission. The fire in the bones of this biographer should kindle heat in Christian hearts made lukewarm by the cosseting of modern western culture.

Timothy G Alford

Here is a book that reveals how pioneering passion when blended with prayer results in the progress of the Gospel. Dick Anderson's story is told with a mixture of honest, humility and reality that is both refreshing and challenging. His insights on the cost of leadership are worth the price of the book alone. However there is much more to learn about the value and diversity of partnership and godly principles for mission in today's world.

Everyone with a heart for Africa will learn from it. All who aspire to lead will benefit from the sway one servant of the King with fire in his bones tells of God's faithfulness in the midst of the battle.

Stanley Davies,
Executive Director, Global Connections

The Andersons have a remarkable story to tell covering quite the most exciting and challenging period of Africa's encounter with the Gospel. Their account straddles the great change from colonialism to independence, pioneering unreached peoples to mature churches emerging and the change of an "old" mission to become "young" and renewed with vision appropriate to Africa's 21st century. So much of what Dick describes I know so well having a range of ministries that almost parallels his!

Patrick Johnstone, WEC

Fire in
My Bones

Dick Anderson

Christian Focus

© Dick Anderson
ISBN 1 85792 676 5

Published in 2001
by Christian Focus Publications,
Geanies House, Fearn, Ross-shire,
IV20 1TW, Great Britain
Cover design by Alister MacInnes

Contents

FOREWORD

In challenging Christians and churches to take seriously their involvement in the Great Commission, I have often used the words of Paul to the Romans, 'It has always been my ambition to preach the Gospel where Christ was not known.' Sadly, there are all too few today who share the Apostle's burning ambition, settling instead for involvement either in their home church or in a place of established ministry overseas. This book is the testimony of one of the exceptions, one of those in whose heart has burned the passion of Paul for those as yet denied access to the message of the gospel.

In his own missionary service, and in his visionary leadership of Africa Inland Mission over many years, Dick Anderson personified this pioneer passion. During his term of leadership, the number of fields in which AIM missionaries served doubled and the priority of the unreached was always at the forefront of the Mission's strategies.

At the beginning of the twenty-first century our world continues to be marked by great inequality. While, in the last century, the advance of the gospel worldwide has been nothing less than breathtaking, nearly one in five of the world's population still lives beyond the reach of the message that needs to be heard and believed in order to inherit eternal life. This inequality is also seen in the fact that the overwhelming majority of cross-cultural missionaries from the western world, around 95%, are working among the reached, or at least those who have access to the gospel.

Yet, increasingly, would-be missionaries want to be assigned to places where there is a measure of security and comfort, and they come from churches who want to have regular reports of dramatic breakthroughs and numerous conversions. That will not likely be the lot of the pioneer missionary, yet the need for them continues to be great.

If this book kindles such a fire in the bones of some of the Lord's people – it will have served its purpose well.

John Brand
UK Director, AIM

PREFACE: PERISCOPIC VISION

Emil lived with a condition called Periscopic Vision. It disturbed his mind and heart in the early years of this century as he preached to the Kikuyu people in the fertile foothills around Mount Kenya. Working in one valley, his eyes wandered to its ridge and questioned about the people in the next. Soon his feet would follow, climbing over the ridge to reach another group of villages. Before long he wondered about residents over the next rise and felt compelled to go to them. When the call came to leave his work in the care of others and consider moving to a neighbouring country, he hoisted his periscope higher, saw the need of people without Christ and consented to go.

Should *we* feel responsible for such people whether they reside in the next estate, in a nearby land, in a distant city slum or away beyond the ranges?

This book is about vision for taking the good news of Jesus across barriers of culture, language, remoteness and discomfort. I have written about parts of Africa and the adjoining islands which I know. Travels in Europe, the Far East and South America have convinced me that certain questions apply to this sort of pioneering elsewhere. What motivates us? How can we approach people who are largely or totally ignorant of Jesus Christ? Should we expect danger, disappointment and delay? Do we risk lives – our own, our families' or colleagues'? How do we face the unceasing hostility of evil spiritual powers?

God's kingly grace arches over this story from beginning

to end, working through fallible servants whose very frailty forces them to depend on him.

I am especially grateful to my wife Joan – surely one of God's gentlest and most courageous soldiers – and to our children who have allowed me to tell something of their own tales. They and others have made many helpful suggestions.

We pray for many to raise Emil's periscope. As a boy he came to know Christ. From then on he believed that his new master wanted him to serve in Africa. Towards the end of his life he said, 'Today that desire is a burning fire.'

You can read more about Emil Sywulka in the author's *We Felt Like Grasshoppers*, published by Crossway Books, 1994.

1

FAITH AND FRUSTRATION

The telephone on my rough folding table shrilled. 'That you Doc?' The Adjutant's clipped voice was tinged with anxiety. 'There's been an accident ... chute failure ... Sergeant Smith ... You'd better get to the Dropping Zone.'

As I drove in a small open Jeep out of our tented camp in the Suez Canal Zone I tried to recall the Sergeant – a tall, tough, respected soldier, a member of the boxing team. He called himself an agnostic. Back in Blighty his girlfriend hoped to marry him. Like all the men in the Parachute Regiment he had volunteered and then been carefully checked for fitness and stamina. Small wonder that his feet seldom brought him into my little Medical Inspection Room.

One look at the sprawled figure showed that death had come instantly. The partially-opened mass of canvas, cords and webbing trailed away forlornly from the straps on his back. A heavy kit bag, strapped to one leg, must have brought him down vertically and thudded into the desert floor with the force of a bomb. Blood and brain trickled from an ear. The parachute failure rate at that time was said to be only one in twenty thousand. Smith happened to be that one.

We buried him with full regimental honours. My friend the Chaplain took us through the Anglican service, but the great words did nothing to lift my sorrow. I wondered if the Sergeant would have appreciated, 'I am the resurrection and the life: he that believeth in me, though he were dead, yet shall he live,' and I could not join in the affirmation that he had died 'in sure and certain hope of the resurrection'. Were we not dishonouring our fine soldier by attributing to him a belief which he had rejected? While a solitary bugler sent the strains of *The Last Post* echoing around our sandy parade ground, I recalled how Jesus' thrilling words had meant nothing to me as a youngster because they came packaged in this formal, external religion which claimed to be the faith of our nation.

*****

Church services injected a regular dose of boredom into my childhood. They did nothing to lift the sadness which seemed the norm to my young life. Dad, a highly motivated doctor, served in Mexico (where my sister, Jean, was born), later in Mauritius (where I first saw the light of day) and finally in Nigeria. When I reached eighteen months, he arranged for us to stay in a nursery school in the south of England while he and Mother returned to their work in Africa. After my sixth birthday the Headmistress called Jean and me into her office one day to hear serious news: Daddy had died of a tropical fever. Jean wept, but my eyes remained dry, for I never felt I knew him. Mother came home to struggle at making a small restaurant pay, with Jean and I helping during holidays from our boarding schools. Jean served at tables while I did duty at the sink. Mother could add a spice of fun to any situation – even when customers arrived as we sat down to our lunch and she quickly demanded, 'Give me the ham off your plates; I've nothing else for them.' She insisted on church on Sundays, but the idea of a warm-hearted, loving God was as remote as the concept of a close, caring father.

A sailor first challenged my revulsion against the

hypocrisy which surrounded the religion of my upbringing. I met him as a freshman at Barts (St. Bartholomew's Hospital Medical College, London.) Demobilised from the Royal Navy at the end of the war, Tim Goode qualified for the priority admission given to ex-servicemen. The Navy had trained Tim to dispose of unexploded mines and bombs on the island of Malta. The Germans dropped everything they could on the gallant garrison, so Tim never lacked work. Nerves of steel and, as he said, the hand of God preserved him in many frightening situations. A faith which sustained a man through such danger just had to be real. He set me reading John's Gospel with a sincere desire to know the truth about Jesus. Was this story fiction or reality? If Jesus was not the Son of God as he claimed, then who was he?

But the faith which Tim tried to nurture in me proved fragile. I could see that Tim was special. And so were the other Christians in College. Maybe God had created them with a disposition towards goodness, which I lacked. With a horror of hypocrisy I gave way to doubt, ceasing to claim the title 'Christian'. But I had started attending Westminster Chapel in London and, despite the turmoil of my unbelief, I kept on.

The minister had himself graduated from Barts many years previously. As a brilliant physician on the staff of this renowned hospital and also running a prosperous practice in Harley Street, Martyn Lloyd-Jones' future had seemed assured until he suddenly abandoned his prospects and became a preacher in South Wales. Now, in Westminster Chapel, he delighted many of us with the clinical accuracy he brought to his Bible teaching.

Lloyd-Jones was more than a clinician. He knew God and he understood the human heart. As he led us, week by week, through the Sermon on the Mount I realised for the first time that Jesus had come to call the spiritually poor who grieved for their weakness and who hungered for something better. Previously I always thought Jesus cared only for saints; now I discovered he loved sinners too. He invited me to know God, to become his son by trusting him for forgiveness and humbly submitting to his kingly rule.

Jesus turned me upside-down. I moved into an East London Club for poor children to try to help them also to know the Lord for themselves. Fellowship in the Barts Christian Union fostered a warmth in relationships I had always lacked, while 'The Doctor's' regular preaching led me to a deeper understanding of God's will and ways.

In the Medical College and Church I met students of my age who shared their faith with others. They went further; many were seriously considering using their skills in service to people overseas, particularly in revealing the love and power of Jesus to people who had never heard about him. These enthusiasms surprised me at first, but as my gratitude for his death for me grew, so my determination to serve him developed.

Final exams consisted of a series of written papers, each lasting three hours, and oral tests, when the student was taken first to examine a patient and then into the awesome presence of a world famous physician or surgeon to discuss treatment. Convinced I had failed, I could hardly believe my eyes when I saw my examination number on the pass list. My training had been mostly theory. It changed quickly in my first job.

In the casualty department of the Metropolitan Hospital, Hackney, my patient needed penicillin. I vaguely remembered learning a dosage formula based on body weight but, with my pen poised over the prescription pad, the details escaped me. I looked up at the experienced nurse who was helping the patient dress and enquired in desperation, 'Sister, what dose is normally given in this hospital?' Without even a smile to embarrass my ignorance she replied, 'two cubic centimetres'. And I wrote it down.

I enjoyed my first year of hospital practice among London's poor, although we were often kept at it for eighteen hours in the day, besides being on call at night. Soon I had to confront the question, 'What does Jesus want me to do next?' The government still insisted that all young men join one of the armed services for two years training. Medical missionary service was recognised as a valid reason for exemption. An elderly minister implored me to consider relieving his son-in-law for a period of leave from a hospital in Kenya. It seemed sensible, but I could not be sure. I phoned Dr Lloyd-Jones for his advice. 'Why not offer your services,' he said; 'and let the Mission decide if you are suitable?'

D. M. Miller, the Secretary of the Africa Inland Mission, invited me to join a house-party he was hosting at a big conference in Keswick. I thought he would jump at my generous offer. I told him, 'I might stay on when the doctor returns. If not, I can do my army service at that time.' His eyes searched me, 'Dick, are you sure God is calling you to go?' I went back to my room to pray. Two years in the Army seemed such a waste of time compared with working in a mission hospital. I told God I wanted the missionary option but he quietly seemed to say, 'Not yet.' Perplexed and disappointed, I had to leave the Lord to show me how I could best spend time in his service.

Three months later a balloon lifted a large basket off the RAF airfield at Abingdon. In it four frightened fellows with parachutes strapped to their backs watched the ground grow small beneath their feet. An instructor tried to raise our spirits by commanding us to sing *Deep in the heart of Texas*. Upward movement ceased. Suddenly he screeched in my ear, 'Red light on, stand in the door!' I took a trembling step and grasped the sides of the awesome gap. 'Green on ... Go!' and he gave me a mighty shove in the backside. To my surprise the canopy opened in seconds and, drifting down after me, came the words, 'The sage in bloom is like perfume, deep in the heart of Texas.'

******

The Army used the 16th Independent Parachute Brigade as an efficient and highly mobile fire fighter. In 1953, when I took up my posting as Medical Officer to the First Battalion, Egyptian resentment simmered against British control of the Suez Canal and threatened shipping lanes to East Africa, India and the Far East. For many months the 'Cherry Berry Boys' (the Army's politer nickname for the Paras, based on their red berets) camped along the western bank of the busy waterway, spilling over into the desert around the town of Ismailia. Our role developed into a dull policeman's duty. Egyptian guerillas challenged us to constant watchfulness, but in the camps, surrounded by an ocean of desert, boredom posed the greater threat. Commanders fought this with vigorous training, much of it on military exercises.

One exercise involved trucking the whole brigade for two hundred miles in darkness. Each driver painted the rear differential of his lorry white, just visible to the driver behind him but to no-one else. I was sent with an ambulance to provide first aid if needed beside the railway line just north of the town of Suez. After midnight the long convoy began to trundle past. A train crawled towards us from Suez at the same time as a lorry approached the crossing. The truck driver's eyes, locked on the white splash of paint in front, didn't noticed the approaching engine until too late. Panic-stricken, he leapt out of his cab moments before the leviathan picked up the lorry and tossed it to one side. The driver escaped.

The next incident ended in tragedy. Five airmen, unassociated with our exercise, careered past in an open sports car singing drunkenly at the tops of their voices. An hour later a military policeman arrived on his motor-bicycle to call us to the accident a mile away – two RAF lads dead and three comatose.

Drink also did something for the bored. Our men rightly prided themselves on their deportment on the battlefield and parade ground, but they boasted too of their prowess in drinking. In the Officers' Mess I quickly discovered a trap for the unwary Christian. Someone buys a round of drinks. Then a second person offers the group a drink. By the time your turn arrives, several people are already drunk. Do you break convention and refuse to buy a round, or do you add to their drunkenness? Inevitably a Christian feels isolated or compromised. I experienced both. There were other compensations. Long, free afternoons gave plenty of time for rugby, swimming and hockey; or else, in the quietness of my tent, I enjoyed studying the New Testament with the aid of a correspondence course from London Bible College. Missing the warm fellowship I had known in the CU and at Westminster Chapel, I once travelled fifty miles in search of another person who shared my faith. Reading the Bible together and praying was like a cool shower on a hot day.

The Air Force dropped us for an exercise in Cyprus. Next

we jumped over Jordan and, when we had completed our war games, the Arab Legion offered us two lorries for a trip to Jerusalem. Walking where the Lord had once lived and preached brought the Bible alive, but immense cathedrals, icons, lamps and a mosque built on the site of the temple where Jesus once taught, spoiled it for me. I felt more at home in the fields outside Bethlehem wondering how the shepherds felt when the angels announced the Lord's birth.

Another safari took us by road into the Sinai peninsula giving us a chance to visit St. Catherine's monastery, home of a fourth century manuscript of the Greek Bible, and to climb Gebel Musa, where many think that God gave Moses the law. One monk had spent his adult life building a stairway up the mountain. At death, monks were buried in the small cemetery which had room for only four coffins. When a newcomer arrived, the oldest was dug up and stacked with his predecessors in a shed. A heap of skeletons testified to the army of monks who have worshipped God in this remote place down through the centuries. What motivated them? Were they trying to earn salvation or to respond to God's grace by grateful service? I could not tell, but their dedication challenged me to seek God's will for my own life in loving response to his kindness.

An opportunity for discovering the next step in this plan soon came. East African soldiers spent two years in the Canal Zone with the Pioneer Corps. Hearing of a ship scheduled to return a large group to Kenya, I asked for a lift. My C.O. agreed to a month's leave. When I saw the *Charlton Star* tied up in Suez I wondered if I had made a mistake as she listed heavily to one side! With a full load she crawled down the length of the Red Sea. In Aden the crew mutinied. After two weeks we reached Mombasa, and the ship's doctor suggested I accompany some patients to Nairobi by train with the help of two friendly orderlies. The doctor warned me that one of the sick suffered from acute hysteria.

Our long train snaked out of Mombasa at 5 mph, climbing slowly on to a dry plain which had spelled life-threatening thirst to early explorers and missionaries. Whoever established priorities for traffic on the line rated us low that night, halting our train for an hour or two at every opportunity. Well after midnight we reached Voi and the men all asked if they could get out to stretch their legs. Two hours later they climbed aboard and we slowly drew away. The two orderlies rushed into my compartment and cried, 'He's gone! The madman has left the train!' I remembered lions that consumed many workers at the turn of the century, when British engineers braved hostile tribes, tropical diseases and wild animals to lay 582 miles of track through untamed bush from Mombasa to Lake Victoria. Wondering what chance my patient would have against the king of beasts, I pulled the communication cord to halt the train. Nothing happened. I leant out of the window and vainly shouted, 'Stop!' Our train chugged on through the African night. After an hour we crept alongside another dark platform and I roused a slumbering stationmaster who telephoned the Railway Police in Nairobi. Anxiety spoiled my enjoyment of a first sight of giraffe, zebra, ostrich and wildebeest as we approached the city at midday. As soon as I had been relieved of my charges, I found the Railway Police office. They said, 'Oh yes. We sent out a patrol and it picked up your man walking along the line towards Nairobi.'

My short stay in Kenya gave time for meeting many fine Christians. I specially enjoyed celebrating Christmas with believers at the AIM centre in Kapsabet. What a relief to be free of the constant buzz of army blasphemy, free to worship God in peace. I shook my head when they enquired if I was thinking of missionary service and replied, 'Perhaps later.' Two years in the Army had done nothing to improve my medical skills, and I needed more experience. In Nairobi a fine government doctor took me to King George VI Hospital where I enquired about job opportunities. The Medical Superintendent said, 'Come for a year. We'll give you lots of experience in medicine and surgery. Then you can decide if you want to work in Africa.'

Back in First Para, I artlessly enquired if they had enjoyed Christmas. 'Yes, we had a great time. Beer flowed freely. The parade ground was covered with drunken soldiers!'

Soon afterwards our government decided to withdraw from the Suez Canal. After a century of massive investment of money and men into Egypt, our Army departed leaving the desert to devour our camps, while sand swallowed huge stocks of old military equipment. My time was up; I was glad to escape from an apparently meaningless stint in an unwanted relic of empire. I returned to 'civvy street' and applied for the Nairobi job. Long afterwards I thanked God for those two years of discipline in the desert, for they proved part of his unerring preparation for my future service.

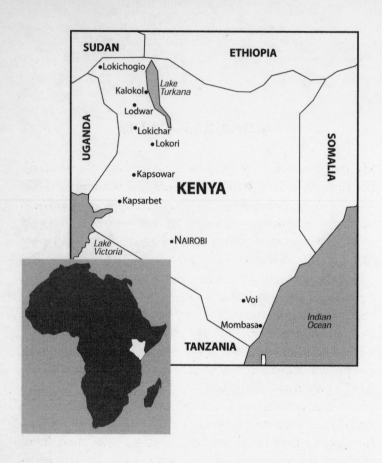

2

A DOUBLE CALL

My daily round of Ward 7 at King George VI Hospital, Nairobi, seemed odd at first. Instead of the normal wide African smile in response to my greeting, a sullen face would turn away in silence, and a pair of handcuffs rattle where a wrist tugged at its attachment to the bedstead. Here and there rifle-armed policemen stood guard over the patients. The prisoners, Kikuyu calling themselves Mau Mau, had rebelled against the British Colonial Government. Some had been captured in the dense Aberdare Forest where they lived in gangs, ready to raid an African village or a European farm, while others had fallen sick in the huge prisons and internment camps, where the security forces kept many thousands.

Out on remote farmsteads white settlers moved with their pistols ready for instant use. Even so, ninety-five died, often brutally cut to pieces by workers they had known and trusted for years. Africans suffered more: 13,423 lost their lives, many of them courageously refusing to swear vile oaths because of their faith in the Lord Jesus. Mau Mau cells operated in the large village for hospital employees which was situated alongside our hospital. A senior nurse, called Gibson, ran an evening Bible study every week and kindly invited me to join. When it was over, the brothers always said, 'We will escort you home; it's not safe for you to walk alone here.' They did not realise that the same risk applied to the walk to Gibson's home in the dark before the meeting, and I didn't like to jog their minds. Fear always tingled down my back as I imagined terrorists eyeing me with their fingers grasping razor-edged choppers.

Gibson's group typified the work of God in those troubled days. Across the city and out in the Kikuyu Reserve, churches filled as people faced the decision, Mau Mau or Christ? My own chief, an orthopaedic surgeon, invited me to speak at his children's service in the Anglican Cathedral. I went expecting a small meeting, but found myself in a pulpit facing hundreds of eager listeners. In the prisons and camps too, many turned to Christ to find forgiveness for horrible crimes. Disillusionment, despair and danger fertilised the soil for the gospel seed.

My surgical boss, understanding my need to gain experience with the possibility of work in an isolated area later, gave me many opportunities and valuable teaching. After the famine of fellowship in the Army, I found a feast in Nairobi – churches of all races welcoming any visitor, lively students learning to live their faith in the hospital's training school, and friendly missionaries coming and going to their guest house across the road from my home. They presented a perplexing array of challenges for future service: a pioneering doctor suggested work among Muslims in Aden; another took me on an extensive trip to visit clinics he supervised throughout Kenya, explaining all the openings for doctors in the Africa Inland Mission (AIM); and an Anglican leader asked me to consider an urgent need at the Kenyan coast. I prayed about each, and felt drawn to none.

Tom and Ruth Collins arrived at the guest house in a dusty Jeep. Peering through two thick lenses which magnified his eyes to the size of grapes (his cataracts had been removed in childhood), he talked about a northern tribe, 'AIM wants to take the gospel to the Turkana. They live tough nomadic lives in a semi-desert half the size of England, so harsh that the Mission director questions whether white people can live there.' He chuckled as he went on, 'The District Commissioner forbids any white women to enter his area. We think the approach should be medical and want to train a Turkana who recently professed conversion at a hospital outside his home district.' Tom himself lived among the Pokot people, bordering on the Turkana Tribal Reserve. He had often walked for weeks at a time through south Turkana, seeking to learn the language and serve the people, until a rheumatic heart, grown to the size of a rugby football, forced him to travel on wheels.

I enquired around, 'If a physical wreck like Tom can do so much, why not others more healthy?' I was due for a final week of leave at the end of my year's contract in the King George VI, and I asked Tom if he could plan a trip around Turkana at that time. As we crawled over deeply rutted roads or struck across country guided only by distant hills or a tree-lined riverbed, I learnt the answer to my question. Tom talked about his time in the Army, 'They graded me C3 because of my heart, but that does not mean much to a God who could raise Christ from the dead.' He succeeded through dauntless faith and dogged perseverance, both of which he regarded as God's gifts. If others believed (however feebly) in the same God, they too could survive in a hostile environment.

In those few days I saw something of the plight of the Turkana people. We paused in a trackless desert place to ask directions of an old man. His solitary garment – a dirty piece of black cloth knotted over one shoulder – slapped in the wind against his desperately thin body. He squinted at us through eyes running with infection, and for a few moments

27

could not understand the question of our interpreter. His mind seemed dazed. Eventually he waved a hand in the direction he thought we needed and said, 'Hunger is eating me; give me food.' In the months to come his image remained with me: a picture of deprivation in every area of human need – physical, mental and spiritual – in a district half the size of England.

In London I visited the AIM office again. I told the Home Secretary about the godly people who had presented challenging needs, making me feel guilty that, when I was available, I did not jump at the opportunity to serve.

The wise old man warned me, 'Dick, the need is not the call; you could fit any number of mission slots, but you need to hear God's directions.' Tentatively I mentioned the Turkana. He let me talk about this tribe of over 120,000 in a remote, barren wilderness, denied the help of either doctor or preacher. He listened and then asked, 'Do you think God wants you to work among them?'

'Why yes,' I replied; 'but I doubt whether the Mission would allow me to go.'

'Probably not to begin with,' he cautioned. 'But if God wants you there, the Mission will not stand in your way.'

I wondered how the Mission Council would react to my second offer of service to AIM, having turned me down three years before. They accepted me, but with a condition, 'We think you need a year at London Bible College.' My pride took a blow. Did they discount my years of Bible teaching from Dr Lloyd-Jones, my sweat poured out on correspondence courses, and my bits of teaching ministry in Nairobi? However, I agreed, and within a few days received a letter from the College to say that my fees had been paid by the AIM Chairman and 'please report next Monday'.

London Bible College opened up a new world of understanding. Although housed at the time in a number of shabby terraced houses in Marylebone, the insistence on academic excellence and practical relevance in all biblical study convinced me that I had scarcely begun to know God's Word. At the end of one year, I wished I could have stayed two more.

As well as thumbing diligently through the books, we enjoyed plenty of fun. A tutor in charge of residential students insisted they wear ties to the evening meal. They obeyed, but omitted to don their shirts. A doctor friend visited me and I took him sailing on Regent's Park Lake. As he had never handled a yacht, I took command (on the strength of a week on the Norfolk Broads with Tim Goode long before). I set the sail to catch every breath of the scant wind. Suddenly a gale blew and slapped the canvas down to water level. The yacht righted itself, but not until it had taken too much of the lake on board. We stood there, laughing helplessly as the water level slowly rose around us. Two men in a rowing boat saw our increasing predicament and sped to our aid. As soon as they drew alongside we both leapt, but we sank the rowing boat too!

As I prayed for the Turkana and read all I could find about them, the conviction deepened that God wanted me to serve them. I pondered some words of a missionary at Keswick, 'The call of God is a conviction which increases in the light of further knowledge until it becomes a straight issue of obedience or disobedience.' A college friend asked, 'What will you do if the Mission refuses to send you to the Turkana?' I felt so confident that I replied, 'They won't. God has given me a double call: to AIM and to Turkana.'

3

TURKANA: A CLOSED LAND

Six powerful cylinders purred as my new Jeep carried me
and a load of rudimentary medical supplies through a forest
of immense cedars in western Kenya. The road reached its
high point at nearly 8,000 feet, where a small monument
reminded us of the engineer who, thirty years before, died
while cutting the route. A flash of black and white turned out
to be a family of colobus monkeys swinging high in the
branches. A few round, grass-roofed huts, surrounded by
waving maize, signalled the end of the trees as the earth track
swung round a bend to reveal a new church looking down on
the line of mud-walled shops which formed a little town called
Kapsowar.

Only a couple of months had passed since AIM leaders in
Nairobi welcomed me. Immediately I realised I had joined a
large family. Old pioneers mentioned their years of praying
for the Turkana and promised to continue. An American
couple, Paul and Dorothy, gave me a home for two months
of Swahili study. Mission leaders augmented my savings so
that I could purchase a Jeep and, to my surprise and joy,
encouraged me to start as soon as I felt ready, under the
watchful eye of Tom. Stanley, in charge of a hospital at
Kapsowar, said, 'Come and stay with me. Kapsowar will be
a good safari base for Turkana and you can get some
experience in the hospital between trips.'

Now I drove slowly past the buildings of Kapsowar
hospital and school, strung out along a ridge which led me

31

up to the doctor's bungalow. Across a green valley to the west a mountain, clothed in forest, rose to a domed summit, while in the other direction a steep escarpment dropped thousands of feet to the Kerio River. At dawn, if the mountain mist permitted, I could see the jagged outline of Mount Kenya 250 miles away etched against a red-streaked sky by the rising sun. Turkana might be hot and harsh, but cool Kapsowar provided a beautiful contrast.

In 1956 the British colonial government kept a tight control on all strangers wanting to enter Turkana. Some senior officers argued, 'Foreigners will exploit these people; missions will disrupt their way of life.' They insisted that no-one enter this outlying district without a special permit from the District Commissioner (DC) – issued only when he was satisfied with the reason for visiting. I sent a letter to the official and waited, wondering how we could disarm official prejudice. Could God, who had so clearly called me, open this closed door?

I got to know some young Turkana men who had found work in Kapsowar. Driven from their homes by hunger, they had fled to the mountains in search of food. As an impoverished group in a foreign tribal area, they clung together and welcomed a missionary with a special focus on their people. In their insecurity they listened to Jesus, the friend of the poor. And they began to teach me the rudiments of their language. One of them named Ewei (because his mother bore him in the shade of an Ewei Tree – the Acacia thorn) had stood up in church before I arrived and announced that he intended to receive Jesus as his Saviour. He now asked if he could travel with me in Turkana – as a paid Christian brother.

At last the DC replied to my application. Yes, I could

visit temporarily, but I had to go first to his office in Lodwar township. Ewei and I set off in high spirits for Lodwar, 400 miles north of Kapsowar, prepared to wait for God's guidance about our next step after meeting the DC. The road ran almost level through a strip of Uganda and then suddenly cut downwards thousands of feet, down a jagged zigzag across the face of a mountainous escarpment. At the top a notice displayed a crude skull and crossbones and the statement, 'Private burial ground for reckless drivers.' Halfway down another underlined the official reluctance to welcome outsiders, 'This is an Outlying District. Entrance forbidden without a licence from the District Commissioner.' Most of all the oven-like temperature which enveloped us as soon as we reached the low, sandy plains would have sent us scuttling home if we had been less sure of our purpose.

Several times we met Turkana people along the road. We stopped, played Turkana messages on an old gramophone a missionary had given me, then I spoke in faltering Swahili while Ewei interpreted into Turkana with dramatic confidence. 'The words are good; yes very good,' they usually responded; 'but hunger is eating us' and here someone would pinch up a fold of skin to show how thin he was. 'Give us food ... or money ... or a shirt.' And on we ran over a badly corrugated road to stop at the next clutch of people. At last we settled for the night outside Lodwar, pestered first by girls demanding money and pointing to my trouser pockets, then by mosquitoes, thirsty for my blood, and finally by unseasonal drizzle.

I slept uneasily. Other missionaries had come this way on the same quest. One had lived for a short while in Lodwar and then settled for a few weeks at a group of wells in the West. Tom had tramped miles through the scorching desert, preaching the Word and living off the land in conditions of extreme hardship. Yet, when each came to ask permission to establish an ongoing work, their applications were rejected. First the people were suspicious, 'The foreigner will deprive us of water,' they complained, 'and he will take our children into his school and then who will care for our flocks?' Later the government doubted the Mission's ability to establish adequate homes and institutions in a country so remote and barren. I wondered in my troubled sleep, 'Why should the simple offer of some health care make a difference now?'

A bugle playing Reveille roused me just before dawn. We reloaded the jeep and drove between three shops of corrugated iron which comprised the town's commercial centre. Then the road ran on past ranks of thatched houses for Kenya Police, a prison crowded with Mau Mau detainees who scowled at the sight of a white face, up a short ramp and into the square, lined by white-painted stone buildings and dominated by a Union Jack. At the far side we pulled up outside the office of the DC.

The elderly Commissioner received us with great courtesy. Yes, we could travel wherever we wished in Turkana apart from the northern border where tribes from Ethiopia and Sudan clashed with the Turkana. 'You can have six months here so that the Turkana can see what you have to offer. Then I will call them together. If they want you to remain, you will stay; if they say "No", you will go!' On leaving his office I met a Prisons Officer who kindly offered me a cup of tea. On hearing the purpose of my visit he said, 'The DC doesn't want missionaries here. I wouldn't give much for your chances of success.'

We turned south, crossed a wide river bed, lined by palms, and headed into haze. Our well-pounded road of the previous day had given way to a single pair of recent vehicle tracks, and sand was already drifting across even these, leaving us to guess anxiously about the route ahead. Desert surrounded us, shimmering in the fierce midday sun. Frequent dry watercourses with step-like banks slowed us to a crawl while their powdery sand grabbed at our wheels and threatened to halt us altogether.

By early evening, when we had covered sixty miles, tall acacias signalled the next watering point, Lokichar. We parked in shade alongside a flock of goats. Every few minutes men drove five or six towards the well. As soon as they caught the scent of water, they rushed to the drinking trough. Thirty feet down the well a woman filled a wooden bucket and passed it to a girl standing in a ledge cut into the sandy side. She bent low to receive the precious burden and lifted it above her head to another. So it mounted from hand to hand until the person at the top emptied it into the trough. Down the bucket travelled to be filled once more and rise again to the rhythm of supple, bending bodies, wet with perspiration, while the men released another clutch of thirsty animals to the trough. Small wonder that, when we set up a little clinic, many came and grimaced as they reached their thumbs round to the lower spine and said with an expressive grimace, 'My back is killing me.'

Everyone seemed to have a physical complaint. If I asked, 'Where is your pain wrong?' a patient often responded, 'The whole body is sick,' and, pointing first to his big toes, ran his fingers up his legs and across his trunk to arrive dramatically at the top of his head. Or if I enquired, 'What's the matter?' patients looked at me in disbelief, 'Isn't that why I've come to you? You must find out.' They gladly swallowed my pills and allowed me to squeeze ointment into their running eyes, but mostly they demanded 'the needle': an injection would cure anything. 'No pain, no gain,' seemed to be their motto. Although we erected a small tent for more private examinations, of necessity we worked mostly in public. A man must show no sign of discomfort. If one came with a toothache, he disdained a local anaesthetic. Ewei sat him on a box, stood behind him and grasped his head against his own body while I held the jaws apart and wrestled a pair of forceps on to the offending member. If he so much as flickered an eyelid, the audience would collapse in laughter. Usually he would sit through the ordeal without the least movement.

The Turkana have been well schooled in endurance. Pain meets a child with his first bout of malaria, pneumonia or dysentery, when parents, desperately concerned to do something for a precious son or daughter, cut into the feverish flesh all over the tender area to cause blood to flow freely and then they rub in ash or camel dung. Or they treat chronic malaria by throwing pebbles into a fire and pressing them into the area over the swollen spleen until a deep ulcer develops, followed by a filthy infection. Whereas a few yellow tablets for malaria, a single shot of long-acting penicillin for pneumonia, and careful hydration for the intestinal upset, could normally produce a rapid cure.

As soon as a number gathered around we sang Turkana choruses: 'Jesus loves me, this I know' or an unrecognisable edition of 'Blessed assurance Jesus is mine' and then produced the gramophone followed by a talk. Everyone understood the drama of the devoted shepherd walking through the night in search of his lost sheep or battling with some wild animal to deliver a goat from its clutches – even to the point of death. Eventually some began to wonder, 'Who is this Jesus who loves us like we love our own animals?'

Others jeered, 'The words are useless; the medicine is water.'

After a few days under the acacias we moved on to the next major group of wells and then to others, always trying to get an idea of the patterns of movement of these nomads and to find a central spot which might serve as a useful site for our base inside Turkana.

Turkana boasts two major rivers, the Turkwel and the Kerio, fed by rains in the remote mountains. In those days, before anyone thought of bridges, we always approached them with a prayer on our lips and the question in our hearts, 'Will it be safe to drive across?' One day, an hour's drive short of the Kerio, I met a five-ton lorry. We often travelled for weeks in South Turkana without seeing another vehicle. So we both stopped for a chat. The trader told me, 'The river is in flood. I waited three weeks on the other bank and just managed to cross this morning.' Looking at my Jeep, a midget beside his monster, he kindly suggested I turn back as I had no hope of crossing for several days. Ewei and I prayed and decided to go on. We reached the river and (with adrenaline pumping) eased the Jeep into the water. Slowly we crept across and then climbed the bank with a triumphant roar from the engine. The water level had dropped two feet since morning, and barely reached the tops of our wheels.

We drove along the north bank among trees until we reached a spot where over the years the river had spread widely, depositing layers of silt, washed down from distant highlands. The people had seized the opportunity to develop millet gardens, unusual in this barren land. But they were unfriendly. A junior chief asked suspiciously, 'Who are you? What do you want?' I told him I brought medicine and good news from God. 'There are no sick people here,' was his curt way of telling me I was not welcome. In fact patients thronged our clinic in their hundreds, but they made it clear they did not want us to stay. Someone even set a curse on us and Ewei was agreeably surprised when it produced no effect.

One lady arrived before dawn and sat among bushes a hundred yards from the tree under which I slept. As soon as I sat up I realised why she had come early. Many hold the superstition that an open sore invites a curse. If someone possessing the ability of an 'evil eye' glances at your ulcer, the condition will worsen and perhaps prove fatal. So you must steer clear of all gatherings of people. I rose, went to her and asked, 'Mama, what's wrong?' Sitting on the ground in typical Turkana posture with her legs straight out in front, she reached forward silently, picked up the lower border of her goatskin apron which covered her lower limbs and lifted it. I saw large sores from hips to feet, suppurating beneath a 'dressing' of camel dung. For a moment I looked with horror and then the stench reached me and I fled back to my camp cot with a prayer on my lips, 'Oh no Lord!' I just felt I could not bear to get involved.

Three days before, in my morning readings I had come to the account of Jesus washing his disciples' feet in John 13 and had wondered at the Lord of the universe performing a filthy task normally reserved for the lowest slave. Now the word struck me, 'I have set you an example that you should do as I have done for you.' Reeling from this powerful challenge I went back to the woman, washed her sores, dressed and bandaged them, injected penicillin and invited her to stay around for a few days. After a week of treatment, she walked home rejoicing in her healing. I think my joy was greater, for the Lord had taught me a fundamental characteristic of his compassionate service to mankind immersed in what to him must be the most revolting filth.

Often a person would call us to see a patient at home. If possible we drove; otherwise we walked, perhaps for several hours in the coolness of night, under a brilliant canopy of stars. If we needed to sleep, a woman usually brought a cowhide for a mattress and a wooden flask full of frothing milk for a meal.

A pattern developed: six weeks safari, followed by three back at Kapsowar for rest, repairs to the Jeep, a chance to pick up some of Stanley's skills in the hospital and to enjoy fellowship. We laughingly formed ourselves into a Bachelors' Club along with another friend.

Returning to Kapsowar after a long trip, our route passed the home of a kindly missionary lady. She welcomed us warmly and invited us to stay for a meal. Poised to ease myself into the first comfortable chair I had seen for a month and a half, she suddenly cried, 'Dick, stop! Don't sit down!' and she rushed into her kitchen. She returned with an armful of newspapers which she spread on the chair. She said, 'Now you may sit.' I sighed for, despite the constant shortage of water on safari, I had thought we managed to keep reasonably clean.

*****

On safari in Turkana Ewei tried to be first at the local wells each morning so that he could fill our cans with crystal-clear water before others arrived to stir up the sand. He usually managed to persuade someone to give us milk for the hot, sweet tea which formed a large part of our diet. Ewei described two categories of patient: the 'dead' and the 'completely dead'. I learnt to enquire if a person's cold, fever, headache, ulcers had 'killed' him (and hence might respond to treatment) or if his spirit had departed. Ewei's friendliness embraced everyone and earned us a hearing as we brought strange words and unusual treatments.

A rollicking sense of humour could relieve weariness. On a rare occasion of rain, a stream began to flow and threatened to fill a favourite well. Ewei borrowed a cowhide whip and pranced in front of the advancing water pretending to threaten it with a thrashing if it refused to stand still. When a middle-aged missionary nurse at Kapsowar told him she was going home to Britain for a few months and might come back with a rich farmer as husband, he collapsed in laughter, rolling helpless on his back. Although he knew that he attracted the ladies, he professed to disdain them with a favourite phrase, 'This thing that is called a woman ...!', followed by an expressive silence.

Illiterate when we met, his alert intelligence taught him quickly. He could usually remind me of a patient I had seen before and the treatment given. He soon revised his own ideas of sickness: for example, tummy rumbles. 'I've got worms inside,' he told me one morning. I responded, 'I'm sorry! Have you seen them?' 'No,' he replied, 'but I hear their voices; they cry out when they have nothing to eat.'

I tried to teach Ewei to read: 'What is this little thing; it's "y"; no, it can't be "y"; oh dear, what is my head like?' He made faster progress in understanding the Bible. I asked him one day, 'Ewei, can you tell me the story I read yesterday of Jesus calming the storm?' He recounted it almost perfectly. Then we learnt together in Swahili, 'All have sinned and fall short of the glory of God.' After he had the words firmly in his mind I said, 'Now tell me what it means,' and he gave me a clear explanation. We often camped at Lokichar where several young men and a woman joined us for these evening sessions and soon some of them professed to love the Lord Jesus. Another class formed among the poor emigrant Turkana at Kapsowar. Would this be the nucleus of a future church when we settled in Turkana? Would some of these very people become church leaders?

One day a young man summoned me, 'Makede calls you.' Everyone except me knew the name and obviously respected its owner. As we approached his home, naked children ran out of their houses, took one look at the Jeep and dashed off in terror to hide in their mothers' skirts. 'This is Makede,' said our guide as an elderly aristocrat stepped out of a low hut. He had once been tall but now his back was bent with arthritis. A short beard of curly white hair framed his lined, leathery face and several columns of short scars across his bare chest showed that he had once slain enemies in his remote warrior past. Solemnly he shook four fingers in front of my face. 'There are four diseases,' he announced and described each. I left him with medicine and returned to my camp. Every day he sent a report. The messages got worse until they told me (with some exaggeration), 'The medicine is good but Makede has died.' I moved my tent to his home and gave him a course of daily injections. Only after his recovery did I discover that he was Turkana's most powerful chief.

The need to settle inside the district became increasingly obvious. Not only could we follow up the embryo Christians more effectively, but we could provide better health care. Tom Collins drove in with two other mission leaders to look at possible sites. They found me looking glumly at a fractured fuel pipe in the Jeep. They took an empty four-gallon paraffin can, found a splash of solder at its join, heated it until it became liquid and then soldered the petrol line together!

41

With my engine firing again, we threaded our way through bushes and across stream beds close to the River Kerio, which, although often dry on the surface, never lacked water deep in its sandy bed. Climbing out of the river we mounted a small plateau looking across a few acres of millet gardens planted where the Kerio had flooded in the past. A gentle breeze eased the blast of heat reflected off the brown rock underfoot. Hills dotted across the scorched plain lifted our eyes to a distant range on the Ugandan border. Someone asked, 'What about this?' With a good water supply, central for South Turkana, and the possibility of a garden, we all agreed it looked promising. Ewei enquired about the name and told us, 'It's called Karoni ke Ekori, which means the Place where the Giraffe Died Giving Birth.' It was, we thought, rather a long name for our centre, and possibly a poor advertisement for medical work, 'Let's call it Lokori – the Place of the Giraffe.'

True to his word the DC called Makede, four other chiefs and three hundred elders to discuss our request. His young representative, the District Officer, explained the benefits we would bring – health, education, employment, development, etc. – and loyally sought to persuade them. An elder (I named him Mr Sour-Face) stood up, waved his hand scornfully towards me and said, 'I know these people. I've worked in the highlands where many of them have farms. Give them this plot and soon they will spread right across our land.' We talked for several hours – but all to no avail. The Officer told me sadly, 'I'm sorry Dick. I must report that they have refused.'

I could not sleep that night and rose from my camp cot to walk across the desert bathed in moonlight. Elders lay scattered in the sand, each covered in a thin cotton square – a sheet by night and a garment by day – and his head cocked up on a wooden support – a pillow by night and a stool by day – with weapons close to hand: a spear stuck into the ground and a hefty club. But where was God? What of all the prayers of his people? I recalled the hospital administrator in Nairobi who had derisively told me, 'You are throwing away your training.' Was he right? I wandered past the sleeping men, my heart crying to God, and could find no rest.

Back in my tent I lit an oil lamp and opened my Bible. A sheet of paper slipped out. Someone had kindly typed verses for me which people had specially mentioned back in Britain. I read, 'This is the word of the Lord ... "not by might nor by power, but by my Spirit"' ... 'See, I have placed before you an open door which no-one can shut ...' All was well; God was in control. I blew out the light, settled on to my sleeping bag and slept like a log.

Next evening the chiefs came to my tent. Makede, wearing a blanket and an ostrich feather, summoned me gruffly, 'Come here and bring a seat.' Having no chair I took a box and sat down. 'You have caused us much trouble,' the senior chief complained. 'We have talked all day and the words have been fierce. Now we have decided ... you can have that site.' What caused the door to swing open? Perhaps a tiny needle in the almighty hand of God.

4

THE WAIT-A-BIT THORN

One arm of a double thorn lies on the ground lifting its partner to jab upwards at a passing sandal, where the point embeds and breaks. Slowly it penetrates the sole until it suddenly stabs the unsuspecting foot. Hence the name: The Wait-a-Bit. Its effect on Jeep tyres is worthy of Satan himself. Your tyre collapses. You remove the wheel, lever the tight cover off its rim, extract the inner tube and pump in air to locate the puncture, only to find that you have now dislodged several thorn tips. You patch all the little holes, run your hand round the inside of the tyre to locate any remaining needle points and carefully dig them out. You pump up the inner tube to check you have missed nothing and then, reassured, let the air out, pack the tube inside its cover, wrestle the tyre back into place and fill it once more with air – but the tyre is as soft as when you began!

A great pioneer missionary, Coillard of the Zambezi, once said, 'Evangelisation ... is a desperate struggle with the prince of darkness and with everything his rage can stir up in the shape of obstacles, vexations, oppositions and hatred, whether by circumstances or the hand of man.'

Convinced that in giving us Lokori as a base God had answered prayer and won a notable victory, we soon learnt that every step we attempted would be viciously challenged. Travel was tough: the government insisted on high standards of building and we had to drag heavy materials two hundred miles over rough tracks, deep ravines and rivers liable to sudden flooding. Strong missionary builders, enduring

45

extremes of heat by day and clouds of mosquitos by night, often succumbed to sickness. Workmen with no education or experience fumbled in their tasks and needed patient training. Spectators thronged to witness the new building drama and, seeing the visitors as a source of every kind of wealth, begged mercilessly from dawn to dusk – '*Nakinay* (Give me) a cooking pot, bread, knives, tools, money, iron roofing sheets, soap, your blanket, your trousers ("But I only have one pair." "That's all right, you can buy another when you drive out for supplies")....' Someone walked away with the starter handle for the only cement mixer within a radius of a hundred miles. Machines broke, cynical colonial officials criticised, witch doctors opposed and Mr Sour-face and his friends continued to snipe. But worse was to come.

At the end of a long trip to Kapsowar, Ewei and I wound our way up the mountains and rounded the bend by the church. A laughing lad waved us down, glad to see the Jeep after six weeks away. I recognised him as one of the more promising Turkana converts and stopped. He opened the door and climbed in. Had I been less weary, I would have realised that he only pulled the door shut without slamming it. As I slowly negotiated the last bend by the doctor's house the door swung open, spilling the young man on to the ground. I braked to a halt and jumped out expecting to see him brushing grass off the seat of his shorts. Instead he lay still on the grass, grey brain tissue oozing from his ear. Numbly I realised he had fallen badly, the force of the blow shooting up his spine to shatter the base of his skull. Within minutes he was dead. I felt devastated at the loss of such a bright young Christian. Quickly the news spread throughout South Turkana that I had been responsible for his death.

My friend Ewei became involved with a married woman

– a major crime in Turkana – so that a chief arraigned him before a court of tribal elders and imposed an enormous fine. The church leaders at Kapsowar, who maintained a great concern for the Turkana work, advised me to look for another safari companion. Kind colleagues at Kapsowar offered Ewei employment and eventually he paid off his penalty. Not long after, Ewei became sick. At operation we found a liver shrunken and scarred, the result of years of undernutrition. He too died. I groaned, 'Lord, for four years he's been my friend and companion; my helper, interpreter and guide. Why take him now?' Again my reputation among the Turkana suffered a knock, for somehow they held me responsible.

One of Ewei's friends was a trader at Lokichar. Talk of Jesus fascinated him. Whenever we camped near his home he and his wife came to read in a halting way, slowly spelling out each word and struggling to grasp the meaning. He listened to the Bible, began to clean up his life and to pray. We wondered if God was developing a leader for the group of enquirers. Government officials noticed his progress too and gave him a job as Sub-Chief. Prestige and prosperity led him into drink and he drifted away. The potential disciples no longer gathered when I visited.

The trader typified almost all the people who appeared to respond in the early years. Of course I knew that only the miracle of God's grace could communicate across the vast gap between my stumbling speech and untuned Turkana ears. Surely, I reasoned, the Lord will shine his light into dark hearts when I faithfully preach and pray and practise pity. I found, however, that if light gleamed for a moment, darkness quickly deadened it; if the word took root at all, thorns throttled the tender growth.

God quietly eased my distress in an unexpected way.

*****

Often in the lonely heat of midday on safari, when many sensible Turkana look for a piece of shade where they can stretch out for a time, I thought about marriage. Prospects looked bleak: the government rule seemed cast in stone – no white women allowed in Turkana. As yet, I had no home of my own; besides, who would share such a rough, nomadic life in a wilderness like this? But apart from my own longing for fellowship and fulfilment, a Turkana church would need the witness of Christian family life. The argument went to and fro in my mind, made more urgent by the attraction of a tall Irish teacher ('five foot twelve,' she always said) who had responded to a clear call of God for missionary service in Africa.

Headmistress of Kapsabet Girls' School in western Kenya, Joan loved to spend her Sundays visiting churches. She used her musical talent to train one of the first school choirs in that part of the country. With a smile for everyone and a quick sense of humour, her pupils called her, 'The Laughing One'. For six months after meeting her in a conference I prayed, 'Yes Lord, I'm prepared to be single for your sake – even though I find it hard – but, when you said, "It is not good for man to be alone," did that include me?' I took the plunge and invited Joan out for a walk and could hardly believe it when she agreed to keep on seeing me.

Missionaries live like fish in a bowl, constantly scrutinised by colleagues, other Christians and a host of unbelievers. A man asked, 'Did you ever see anyone as much in love as Joan Boyd?' 'Ah,' replied his friend, 'you haven't seen Dick Anderson yet!' But one senior colleague who knew Turkana took me aside. He warned me, 'Joan works well in the school situation but do you really believe she can cope with your sort of life?'

Joan too had doubts. She loved the regular programme of an institution with its rhythms of terms and holidays, time tables and duties. Others had negotiated permissions, searched for funds, built classrooms and dormitories, recruited staff, and tackled a multitude of challenges in setting up her school; she preferred the predictability of functioning in a system already established. Although she saw the priority of pioneer advance she shrank from its uncertainties, knowing at that time we had no clear plan for the Turkana work, no government approval, no idea of our future home and hardly any money. The vast difference in climate also made her think twice: I was asking her to exchange cool green highlands for scorching desert.

Having made up her mind Joan never looked back. After we announced our engagement, a cheeky schoolgirl – still needing Joan's help with English tenses – challenged me, 'Who give you permission to take away our Principal?' We could both answer, 'God!'

I brought her to a two-roomed temporary home at Kapsowar built from the trees which clothe the surrounding mountains. Our bedroom was perched on cedar stumps, each capped with metal to prevent ants from climbing up into the house. But millions found their way around the barrier and munched away at our floor, walls and ceiling. Each morning we swept up their leftovers of fine sawdust.

My safari programme meant that Joan often stayed alone at Kapsowar for as long as a month at a time. We both felt the strain of these long separations. Despite wonderful colleagues, Joan longed for a more settled existence. One night, while I was away, the ceiling crashed down around her in bed. On another occasion she was suffering from a painful back when her foot plunged through a weakened plank. Ruefully she lifted her leg to examine the grazes and suddenly realised that the jolt had cured her back!

We asked the Lord, 'What about children for us, Lord? Could they survive in Turkana? Would you provide for their education in remote boarding schools? Would that be fair on them?' When he gave three conceptions in rapid succession, we believed the Lord had answered and we placed each, still unborn, into his hands, begging that he care for them and bring them to know and love the Saviour.

Mary arrived first. Soon after her birth we took a holiday in the lush farmlands to the south where we met a teenage Turkana girl called Maraka who had been introduced to Christ by a godly farmer's wife. The elderly saint told us, 'She really hasn't a chance here. The family is trapped in squalid poverty and the moral climate in the village will be disastrous for a girl of her age.' We asked Maraka, 'How would you like to live with us?' She eagerly consented and her mother, glad for an illegitimate daughter to get a chance to progress, allowed her to leave. At the girl's request Joan helped her shed a heavy goatskin skirt and apron, unwind strings of dirty beads from her neck, bathe and put on a cotton dress. With wonder she said, 'How light it all feels!' At Kapsowar the same awesome sense of God's newness persisted as Maraka joined the Turkana, learning to read and rapidly outstripping them all. We little realised at the time that she would become like a daughter to us and a Christian leader for hundreds of Turkana women.

One morning, while Joan was wondering if she was pregnant again, she read in the book of Samuel, 'She gave birth to a son and they named him Solomon.' Solomon turned out to be Helen! By then we had moved our base, first to the home of Tom and Ruth Collins in the hot Kerio Valley, and then up on to a high mountain ridge to a teacher's small house in a new school complex.

*****

At Lokori, Paul and others were building a home for us which we hoped would endure for many years. We had wanted something small and simple, but the government would only agree to house plans which accorded to their own standards for western personnel. Later, although we often felt that our home placed a cultural barrier between us and the Turkana living in their simple huts around us, we would be grateful for this stipulation. Paul also wrestled with the termite problem. The ants of Lokori, although a different species from those at Kapsowar, possessed the same consuming appetites. A visitor who hung her dress on a chair overnight found only shreds in the morning. So Paul determined that this new structure would contain nothing into which the little eaters could sink their teeth. He bought discarded railway lines and welded them into a solid frame. Then he filled in the walls with cement blocks and the roof with concrete. Louvred windows captured every breath of breeze and cooled us better than a fan. A missionary engineer embedded well rings deep into the dry river bed until they reached water and then installed a pump. We exulted when water surged, copious and clear, out of the pipe at the house site.

We still faced the hurdle of government permits not only for a white woman but also for her babies. In correspondence with a senior government official, our mission leader, Erik

Barnett, wrote with us in mind, 'We normally include families when we send out our workers.' We held our breath, but no objection came back and we thanked our Father.

By June 1961 we decided the house at Lokori was habitable even if not quite finished. We loaded furniture and baggage on to the jeep and I set off on the long drive north, leaving Joan and the two girls to fly in with Missionary Aviation Fellowship (MAF) two days later.

Joan had to contend with builders and painters all the time. To her orderly mind everything seemed chaotic with limited furniture, little cupboard space and supplies lying everywhere. As the only housewife, the task of entertaining fell to her.

By the time we took up residence the local people had grown accustomed to white men. But the arrival of a woman with two babies astonished them. They gazed in – commenting on every activity, exclaiming with wonder at all the paraphernalia of western family life, begging good-humouredly for anything that caught their fancy and, as the afternoon sun cast a dense shadow from the house, lying down on our verandah to sleep, chew tobacco and gossip. Joan had moved far from her orderly life as a respected headmistress.

*****

Lokori averaged five inches of rain each year, but for the two years before our move drought prevailed. Soon afterwards a sudden squall struck, flooding the Kerio beside our house and converting thousands of dry water courses into raging torrents for a few destructive hours. Flocks of skinny goats, weakened by lack of forage, were suddenly swept away and drowned. One wealthy man lost everything.

We watched big trees, uprooted from the river bank, float

past. One stuck on the exit pipe from our well, raising the big steel plate which capped it and allowing it to fill with brown sludge. We had carefully enquired from the local folk about the highest known level of the river in flood and built our little pump house on the bank above it. Now from our home we could see that the walls of the shed had been swept away and the pump itself stood in the midst of a sea of rushing water. For several months we experimented with other schemes. We experienced the disgust of turning on a tap only to see a brown trickle emerge or, worse still, a gurgle followed by nothing. On the other hand, when the scheme worked for a while, a steady flow of clear clean water would make us almost delirious with delight.

Rain revealed weaknesses in our beautiful house. Its iron frame expanded in the intense noonday heat and contracted at night. The relentless process, day after day, produced fine cracks in the concrete roof. Although we painted them with bitumen, heavy rain always seeped into the house. Driven by fierce wind, the rain smote our louvred windows, running upwards to burst through the overlaps and shower into our rooms. We could only pick up our few mats, move furniture away from the windows and wait for the deluge to cease so we could sweep out the mess.

The Turkana lived in homes which were more vulnerable. By day they used their huts as shelters against the fierce sun, while at night they often slept outside around a fire which died down at the same time as the country cooled. Scantily-covered bodies chilled. If rain fell, they stretched leaky hides over their low huts and shivered inside. Chest infections multiplied. Mosquitoes swarmed and a malign malaria swept through the villages.

Even so, everyone loved the rain. Clouds gathered for

several days in advance and we enjoyed the strangeness of needing a pullover in the evening or a blanket at night. A nightjar sang and the Turkana told us it was announcing the imminent rain. Then, after the downpour, frogs massed along the river, filling the night air with croaking chat which Ewei always said was the bulls serenading their mates. After two or three showers, grass seeds, dormant for years, sent shoots up between the brown rocks and spread a thin green haze across the barren land. Cattle grazed, camels and goats found new succulent leaves on the bushes and the desert rose blossomed orange. Animals grew fat; udders, which had been dry for months, flowed with milk; and the Turkana danced long into the night to the rhythm of clapping hands and stamping feet which kept time with sentimental songs about their favourite oxen.

*****

Mostly the nights were hot. Helen, aged four months when we moved, could not adjust to them but roused us four or five times each night with her whimpers. In us insomnia bred irritability, made worse by the mental haze which blotted out our vital early morning times of prayer and Bible reading. We survived spiritually by climbing to the roof when our day's work was over and praying aloud in brief disconnected sentences, blurting out our needs while the stars shone serenely down and the peace of God stole slowly into our hearts. Eventually Joan realised that Helen wanted more food. She tried gently pouring milk between her lips. The baby gulped and pursed her lips for more. Only the jug could slake her thirst and, once that was satisfied, we could all sleep at night.

Australian colleagues, Bill and Margaret, came to share

our house. Bill drove a lorry load of their furniture as far as the Kerio ford two miles away, but decided the water was too deep to attempt a crossing. He walked to Lokori and suggested I help with the Jeep. Little Mary, always ready for excitement, jumped into the cab beside me while several workmen climbed on to the back. We manhandled the load across the river until only a heavy refrigerator remained. I said to Bill, 'I think I could drive the Jeep over.' We tied a rope to the front bumper in case we stuck and needed the men to pull. With Mary standing on the seat beside me, I eased the truck into the river, drove slowly across and climbed the far bank without trouble.

The extra weight of the fridge proved too much for the return crossing, and our wheels stuck in soft sand. While men grabbed the rope to pull, others pushed from behind and I revved up the engine to get maximum power. Suddenly I noticed Mary had lain down, her head on my knee. Glancing at her face I was appalled to see a blue discoloration, which deepened in the few seconds that I watched. Then I saw gas bubbling up through the water which had seeped in to cover the floor of the Jeep and I remembered an ailing exhaust underneath the cab. She stopped breathing. In agony I lifted her out of the poisoned atmosphere and held her through the window, shouting to Bill for help. He assessed the situation immediately, cradled her in his arms and, lowering his lips to cover her mouth and nose, gently breathed into her lungs.

I watched in an agony of suspense. After a few minutes – like an eternity to me – Mary coughed and started breathing again. Soon her colour returned to normal. We drove home where the emotional tension suddenly hit us both as we tried to tell Joan and Margaret about the little girl's close brush with death. We collapsed in tears.

Joan was carrying our third child. Assailed by heat and a multitude of unsavoury smells, nausea troubled her more than during her other pregnancies. At the end of three months, we realised that something else was wrong. Without a manipulation under anaesthetic, she would lose the pregnancy. As Bill and Margaret were nurses I talked it over with them. They agreed that I needed to get Joan to Nairobi for specialist help. But how?

Our Director had insisted on sending a small radio transmitter to us so we could maintain daily contact. It often failed us, and I was not too disappointed when it broke down completely. 'At least,' I thought, 'I'll not need to waste time on it each day.' Now we really wanted it. Bill and I crouched over the radio, desperately twisting its knobs, but it only whistled and squeaked. I decided to drive to the nearest telephone – seven or eight hours away – and call the Missionary Aviation Fellowship.

As I headed south I saw dark clouds massing over the pass through the mountains. I was not surprised to find that a little stream on the Turkana border had swelled. I waded across with water swirling around my waist and I realised my vehicle wouldn't stand a chance. In gathering dusk I walked on towards a government settlement twenty miles away to seek help and was astonished to hear a car approaching, for you could wait a month on that road without seeing another vehicle. A Landrover pulled up. The driver introduced himself as an anthropologist travelling to his camp a few miles north of the river I had just forded. I warned him, 'The Landrover will never make it. Why don't we exchange trucks: you use mine to go on to your camp and I borrow yours?' We arranged to meet at the river next morning and I sped up the pass in heavy rain.

Just after midnight I found a telephone in the first major town in the high farmlands. The pilot's wife answered, 'Hi Dick! Gordon's away but he's due home.... Yes, I'm sure he can make it to Lokori tomorrow.' A sense of relief swept over me as I turned the Landrover round and started homewards. At 10 am, sipping coffee in the anthropologist's camp, I heard a small plane high overhead – Gordon on his way to collect Joan. Her surgery went well and she came home to Lokori. Six months later Donald arrived to complete our family.

God gave us three children under the age of three. We often recalled the confident colonial official who told us when we first settled at Lokori, 'White children cope with this climate for a year or two. After that they sicken.' We too were confident, not in some innate strength in our youngsters, but in the assurance that the God who had called us to Turkana would care for us.

Joan sometimes wished she could have spread the heavy work of raising three youngsters over a few more years, but their closeness in age had compensations. In a remote place with no other children of their own culture, they relished the companionship of each other. Later some other missionary children joined us and became good friends. Prior to their arrival, our three often walked in the bushes beside the Kerio or swam in the muddy water, coming home to hose each other down or soak in a cold bath. They came with us on safari, sleeping in our tent or under the stars, joining in our boisterous hymn singing, quietly watching people react to our preaching or line up for my clinic.

The nearest white people lived a hundred miles north in Lodwar, so travellers often dropped in. The girls jumped up and down with excitement whenever an unexpected plane buzzed us to request that we bring visitors in from the airstrip, but Joan's heart often sank at the prospect of more mouths to feed from scant supplies. We met an interesting collection of people: the Kenyan Vice-President, church leaders, a modern composer, ambassadors from Norway and Germany, rally drivers, many doctors and pastors and others who mistakenly assumed we were lonely. An ambassador, this time from France, offered us two bottles of whisky – assuming we were thirsty.

A lady visitor set her hair in curlers and settled her camp bed on our roof thinking to escape the heat. She had not bargained for Lokori's fierce wind. Her curlers flew across the desert. We wondered what their Turkana finders would think of them.

A good friend who owned his own plane, arrived on Christmas afternoon with a third secretary from the British High Commission who was also a concert pianist. He played our piano while Joan sang. Our friend told Joan, 'I've a present from Ruth.' Joan rejoiced, for she had long encouraged this brilliant man to find a wife. But Ruth's present was a churn of milk, for Ruth was a cow.

*****

The sense of spiritual opposition never left us for long.

Bill Anderson responded to a call from Chief Makede and found that a carbuncle on his back had forced his temperature up. Bill brought him to Lokori where by then we had a small hospital ward with twelve beds. The patriarch stayed for several weeks, and often heard about the love of Jesus. His old scorn softened into a lively interest and, when he recovered, he invited us to hold a monthly clinic in his village.

Back in hospital a patient died. A witch doctor, hostile because of our friendship with the senior chief, rifled the grave and used parts of the corpse to prepare a curse. The spell frightened the old man so that when he became sick again he called the witch doctors instead of us. Their treatment failed and he died.

One day Bill himself came home early from a safari in great pain. Over the next few days his condition deteriorated until we decided to send him to Nairobi. Fortunately the radio now functioned well and we readily contacted MAF. His condition baffled the Nairobi doctors for a time, but eventually they diagnosed porphyria and advised him to return to Australia. The loss of Bill and Margaret seemed like Satan's masterstroke, for they had been such good friends and allies – so caring, tough and able. But God planned something else for them and he was preparing others to work alongside us.

5

THE PATIENT PASTOR

When we moved to Lokori, AIM had 175 missionaries in Kenya serving hundreds of churches. With a passion to spread the gospel, this large family formed a mature base for the new work – providing advice and assistance in a multitude of ways. Our denomination, Africa Inland Church (AIC), clarified her missionary vision and determined to place Kenyan missionaries among people groups still unreached. The AIC sent Peter and Roda Mualuko to Turkana.

The Mualukos lived next to us and Peter and I often travelled together. He taught me to make maize porridge and politely endured the results. Peter asked me to teach him to drive. Nosing the Jeep down a sandy river-bank one day – a procedure normally done with the utmost care – he put a foot on the accelerator instead of the brake and we both cracked our heads sharply against the cab roof.

Peter opened my eyes to an African understanding of the world of evil spirits. After a long clinic and several sessions of preaching, we stretched out on our camp cots and Peter told me about his first contact with Christ. Lying in a hospital bed with a high fever he lost consciousness. Menacing dwarf-sized figures crowded round him announcing, 'You are coming with us.' He awoke briefly, but long enough to tell a fellow patient about the demons. His friend asked, 'Are they greater than Jesus?' and prayed for him. He lapsed into a coma and the threatening spirits returned. He heard another voice, kind and gentle, 'Don't mind their spears; they cannot harm you; just ignore them.' Years later he turned again to the Lord, this time for forgiveness. The Lord Jesus transformed him, giving a fresh power over sin and a new purpose for service.

One hot evening after dark, we sat on stones around the little fire on which we had cooked supper. My shirt-tail hung down over my shorts to encourage air to circulate. Suddenly Peter reached across the fire, grasped my shoulders, lifted me and said in a tone which would not allow contradiction, 'Bwana Daktari (we always addressed each other with great respect) Come!' Astonished at this unusual treatment I slowly rose with his hands firmly controlling my movements. 'Now look,' he said, and pointed to where I had been sitting. A puzzled snake cast its head from side to side wondering why the fire had suddenly become so bright. The pastor told me, 'It was rising between the end of your shirt and your back; and I feared to warn you lest you leap up and it would bite.'

When we settled into Lokori, poverty stalked the drought-stricken land and starvation threatened. The government herded thousands of paupers into famine relief camps, where we visited them. One day we came across the District Commissioner, an ex-colonel, in the largest settlement of five thousand. The Colonel watched the pastor chatting to the people and was amazed to see his love. Other Kenyans he knew, from so-called developed tribes, despised the Turkana. 'I need an honest man to care for these people,' he told me. 'Do you think Pastor Peter would like to live here in Kalokol?'

The Mualukos moved in as drought gave way to heavy rain which poured through their palm leaf roof. Like us, this missionary couple met a culture which seemed very different from their own, they also faced the challenge of a new language. When Roda became seriously sick Peter took her to hospital 250 miles away where three pints of blood saved her life. We doubted if Roda would return, and we knew that Peter would refuse to be separated from his wife for more than a few weeks. On my next visit to Kalokol I heard a shy voice saying, 'Greetings, Bwana Daktari.' I turned and saw Roda's smiling face. No satanic stab could puncture her commitment to the Turkana. Pastor Peter opened a school, assisted AIM people to develop a fishing scheme on the adjoining lake and then, as the poor realised their need for more than food, he introduced them to the Lord. Peter Mualuko became the midwife to the first church in Turkana.

With Kenyan independence in 1963 an African DC, one of Kenya's first successful Olympic athletes, arrived at Lodwar. We called to pay our respects, and Joan wondered if he would remember that she had taught him Scripture at his school in Kapsabet. At that time secondary education was rare in Kenya and students valued their teachers. He recalled Joan's classes with gratitude and asked, 'Why do you not open a church here in Lodwar?' We talked it over with Peter and he decided, 'The Lord has blessed the church here in Kalokol. We now have several leaders; Roda and I will go.'

Lake Turkana stretched for 150 miles along Turkana's eastern border. Famine camps gave way to fishing communities, and many people developed the dignity of caring for themselves. Our Church Council led by Pastor Peter employed a famine relief worker called Paul to develop the fishing scheme at Ile Springs. Soon famine food was no longer needed as the people learnt to feed themselves from the bounty of the lake. Paul preached and then worked with believers to build a church with palm trunks as walls and palm fronds for a roof.

He invited Peter Mualuko to officially open this new

outpost of the AIC. After a service in the cool building we all trudged through deep sand to the lake shore where Peter baptised twenty new Christians. Black shining faces, wet with perspiration from the midday heat, beamed with joy. A one-legged woman parked her crutches at the water's edge and, leaning on a friend, hopped to where the pastor stood in waist-high water. Another, crippled by a badly in-turned club foot, hobbled out to be immersed. And finally an old man's face, wizened by the hardship of poverty, lit up with a broad smile as the pastor asked, 'Are you trusting in the Lord Jesus?' and he replied, '*Acamit lokojokon*' (I accept him completely)! With Peter's gentle push on his chest he plunged down and then, with a firm lift to his back, bounced up again while tambourines shook and the congregation exulted, '*Ngai epidori akingarakin? Ngesi Yesu!* (Who is able to help us? Only Jesus!) *Ngai epedori akiteyar? Ngesi Yesu!* (Who can save us? Only Jesus!)'

Little churches began to form. People came with the baggage of sin and shattered relationships which they handed over to the Lord while we encouraged them to grow in spiritual understanding. But, without either a Christian background in society or the ability to read for themselves, they needed much help. As believers increased, so did the tangles which needed unravelling. We taught God's Word and sought his wisdom. Peter Mualuko became our leader. For hours, often long into the night, he would quietly listen to all facets of a problem and encourage us to find the Lord's solution.

New religious groups hostile to the faith we taught followed us into Turkana, seeking to turn believers away. Often, like needles in our tyres, they punctured new initiatives. With an African government in charge, we needed a respected person to negotiate with officials and to put out fires lit by our enemies. Peter, living in Turkana's main town, undertook this sensitive duty. I often wondered at his patient strength in this thorn-strewn environment.

God brought other allies to fight the battles of his kingdom in Turkana. One midnight I came to an isolated shop, built of mud and sticks and strongly protected with a thorn fence. Seeing a light, I stopped to say hello to the friendly Indian who ran it. He had often asked for medicines and sometimes gave us meals in return. If he chose to eat with us we would watch him draw out a handkerchief, remove two dentures and wrap them before he could tackle his food. Once before on a rainy night I had asked if I could lay out my camp bed and sleep in his place, only to wake in the morning covered with weevils which had invaded my sleeping bag from the sacks of maize piled up beside me. So, although home was still three hours drive away, I determined that I would not repeat the experience.

Mr Patel astonished me. 'I have visitors,' he announced proudly: 'two white ladies ... and you must meet them.' He disappeared to the back of his domain to call his guests and out walked two Finnish ladies clad in their dressing gowns. Anna and Marjaana had come to plant a church on the troubled border between the Turkana and Pokot tribes. They too became firm friends, building a school and hospital which I visited every month.

A Dutch team from the Reformed Church came to our first safari centre, Lokichar, and found our tiny school. They enquired if they could work with us and we gladly surrendered our work there, feeling they had much greater resources for development. Canadian Pentecostals and the Salvation Army followed in other places where we had served. In such an enormous area we reckoned there was room for all, provided they preached faith in the saving death of the Lord Jesus and taught believers God's Word. As the years went by, many young believers, trained in our AIC schools, became mature pastors and teachers for other denominations.

*****

Nothing tested our perseverance as much as separation from our children. The dreaded day of Mary's departure to boarding school in the cool highlands came all too soon. She seemed like a wee waif when we left her sitting on a bed watching other children taking tearful farewells of their parents. A mile down the road I needed to stop to comfort her weeping mother.

Over the years these farewells did not grow easier; each was a sort of emotional surgery. The joy of welcoming the youngsters home quickly dispersed in the knowledge of coming separation. Donald, the youngest, found it hardest. He often cried, 'My tummy hurts' a day or two before departure and we knew the great wrench had arrived again.

We had to learn that our children belong to God. We treasure them but he loves them more; we train them but he is the better teacher. We sensitively commit each into his compassionate hands, and he cares both for them and for us. As they left for school and we remained, we found the words of Jesus true, 'No-one who has left home or wife or brothers or parents or children for the sake of the kingdom of God will fail to receive many times as much in this age and in the age to come, eternal life' (Luke 18:29, 30).

God comforted us in many ways, not least by his financial provision. From the earliest days of AIM, missionaries determined to present personal needs to our Father in heaven and to him alone, convinced that he could spur people to give. Hudson Taylor, the great missionary to China, taught us the principle, 'Learn to move men through God by prayer alone.' Initially friends realised the expense of boarding education and gave generously. After Kenya became independent, we received a surprising letter from the British High Commission in Nairobi. In reviewing development aid to former colonies, the UK government discovered that some of her citizens, working as doctors in Kenya, had left because of the difficulty of finding adequate school fees. Her Majesty's Government planned to remedy this in two ways: a salary supplement to cover most of the fees and, for children studying in Britain, return air fares for school holidays three times a year. This generous provision continued right through secondary school for our three children.

*****

Joan found an absorbing interest eased the pain of partings: the language. She had much more time for Turkana study after the youngsters left for school. Many of us experience language learning as a grind – essential but demanding. Joan actually enjoyed it. Her musical ear quickly picked up tones and cadences; her organised mind appreciated the challenge of sifting and sorting mounds of information, and her outgoing temperament never shrank from trying out new phrases on her African friends. At Kapsabet she had learnt Nandi. During our months at Kapsowar she tackled first Swahili, with its Bible and extensive literature, and then the much greater challenge of unwritten Turkana. An early visitor, hearing Turkana for the first time, thought it sounded like a person gargling. From her first safari into Turkana Joan started analysing the language: writing down words, wrestling with tenses and genders, listening for tones – all the time practising and asking people to correct her. For a while she taught in school, and then, while our growing children demanded much of her attention, she had little opportunity for study or teaching. When they left she could give herself to it.

We laughed when someone suggested that African languages were simple, lacking the full vocabularies and complex structures of 'more developed peoples'. Joan produced *A Turkana Grammar for Beginners*, to help fellow missionaries. She headed one page, 'A Lesson on Anatomy', and went on to list sixty-three body parts and that was just the start! Even children knew the name of every plant and bird. Verbs fascinated her. When telling a woman to jiggle (*kikinikinak*) her fretting baby on her knee or to whisk (*kikolakolak*) the porridge, the words were was so expressive Joan could almost see the infant bouncing up and down or smell the cooking gruel.

Love of languages may be the most important asset of a translator, but Joan knew she needed skills as well. Three months at the Summer Institute of Linguistics opened up realms of understanding which helped her to gather, collate and analyse the vernacular. When she became immersed in translation, she received enormous help from the Bible Society which arranged a workshop in Nairobi for six weeks and also linked her with invaluable consultants. One tense was so complex that it eluded her for years – in fact, she never fully understood it. A visiting professor of linguistics puzzled over it for a few hours and finally exclaimed, 'I think we need to pause; insanity is round the corner!'

I understood the frustrations of translation when I walked home for my lunch, savouring the feeling of the sun soaking into my back to the very bone. I heard Joan's despairing exclamation, 'Abomination of desolation!' When I went inside she flung questions at me, 'What does it mean? How do you translate it into Turkana?' Although she loved these conundrums, they also exasperated her when she could not find an answer. How do you say, 'as white as snow' to people who have never seen the cold stuff? Our words like 'heart', 'mind', 'repentance', 'faith' and a host of others have no real equivalent. Turkana minds do not ponder the abstract; they think and speak in concrete terms – forthright, vigorous and dramatic. To speak of 'the belt of truth' sounded like nonsense in Turkana ears for a belt has only one function. She read to her Turkana informant, 'Abraham rejoiced to see my day....' He laughed, 'How can a man see a day and especially one so far in the future?'

To resolve these mysteries she always depended heavily on the local people themselves. One of the best was Maraka who had moved with us to Lokori. By then she had grasped a fair knowledge of the Bible and could teach other children. With her quick intelligence she helped Joan with language data thus allowing her to attempt a preliminary analysis. As Joan's understanding developed, Maraka helped prepare the *Grammar* and then to translate parts of the New Testament. Whenever they completed a few chapters Joan called together a committee to scrutinise every syllable, trying to make sure of accuracy in translating the original meaning, and of relevancy in communicating it into Turkana idiom.

Fumbling as we were to relate to Turkana culture, Maraka opened our understanding and, like Ewei before her, created bridges for the gospel into dark hearts. After three years of Joan's tuition she entered Bible School where she acquitted herself well with students from a school background of seven years. Three years later she returned to teach in Lokori Primary School and eventually to marry our Christian headmaster. They moved to Kalokol and became leaders in the church.

Occasionally we drove the one hundred miles to Lodwar to see Peter and Roda. Crawling up the rocky track, we would pass the new church and approach his small home, built of corrugated iron. There we found him at prayer on the verandah with his Bible open. Once, discussing spiritual warfare, he told us, 'A lad graduated from Bible College and he asked his teacher to tell him in one word how to succeed in ministry. The teacher replied, "I will give you not one word but three: vumilia (persevere), ... vumilia, ... vumilia."'

6

FLAMES FLICKER AND FLARE

Isaiah knew about perseverance. Looking out on his own scene he cried, 'Oh that you would rend the heavens and come down, that the mountains would tremble before you! As when fire sets twigs ablaze and causes water to boil, come down to make your name known to your enemies' (Is. 64:1, 2). After about ten years at Lokori it seemed as if we produced enough heat to warm the water but never sufficient to boil it. While God was blessing Pastor Peter's work in Kalokol and Lodwar, we could see little progress in ours. Worshippers came to our airy church on Sundays, and some attended midweek services. Hospital patients listened to our daily message and sang Turkana hymns with joy; people welcomed us to their homes and appreciated our prayers. Children thronged our school and a few people professing faith, received baptism. But often a fire we thought God had lit in some heart burnt for a while, flickered and then fizzled.

For sure we could see God's kingly reign in a multitude of ways. Surrounded by gross physical need, we made some progress in establishing a hospital to cope with thirty inpatients. Although not all who came seeking healing found it, many did and went away thankful for health. We longed that they find forgiveness and new life as well; few did that, and of those few, most fell by the wayside.

God displayed his power in healing, often by what seemed like miracles. Epetet came to hospital squirming in agony – the result of an enlarged prostate gland. Before we could remove it, a surgeon friend arrived by plane. He asked, 'What operation do you perform?' When I told him, he smiled, 'A bit out of date, Dick! Let me talk you through the modern method.' Through a needle in the spine I injected anaesthetic and then John explained the procedure, step by step. Immediately after John's departure next day, bleeding started. Back on the operating table I unpicked the stitches and searched for the erring artery. The nurse said, 'Pulse is bad ... I can't get a blood pressure ... He's stopped breathing!' Silently we all cried to God. I asked the sister to inject adrenaline. The vital signs returned, faintly at first and then with increasing strength. Bleeding ceased and he survived! I implored relatives to give blood but they only sneered and a missionary provided the priceless pint. When I told him he had died but God had heard our prayer and restored him, he laughed. God's power and pity left him unmoved. 'O Lord,' we asked, 'why do you work one miracle and deny the other?'

Somali traders came from afar to establish shops at Lokori. Many suffered from recurring tonsillitis and asked for surgery. I always shied away from tonsillectomies, hating the tide of blood welling up from the depths of the throat. An eye surgeon, Philip Morris, had perfected this skill before concentrating on his speciality. When he came to us for a list of eye operations, I asked if he would like to take out some tonsils as well. His fame spread. Before his next scheduled visit, Somali people came, one from as far away as Tanzania. At the last moment Philip cancelled, leaving me to attempt the procedure. Thanks to Phil's previous lesson, all went well. We treated many Somalis for all sorts of conditions and some became good friends. But none found faith.

Akiduri's husband traded maize and tobacco around Turkana, using donkeys as his vehicles. One tried to run away. Akiduri grabbed at the rope, caught it, but fell heavily on her left side. A sickening pain stabbed her chest like a knife as she lay groaning on the ground. When we got her into Lokori several hours later, she was bleeding internally from a big malarial spleen which was obviously lacerated.

My surgical textbook told me that unless I removed the spleen the patient would certainly die. With no anaesthetic machine, no proper facilities for blood transfusion and no surgeon within two hundred miles who had ever removed a spleen, I decided to wait. But it was time wasted. We wheeled her to theatre and risked a high spinal anaesthetic. It took well and we proceeded with the operation, finding blood still running from a rent in an angry, cherry-coloured spleen. Recurrent malaria had bound it to all the surrounding structures with thick bands of unyielding scar tissue. To dissect it free would have taken a long time, and her condition was deteriorating by the minute. By packing a towel around the spleen we could control the bleeding, but each time I attempted to remove it the flow started again. Finally we left the cloth around the rent and led the end out through the skin. As long as it remained in place all might be well, but it must be removed in forty-eight hours, and then she would be liable to further bleeding which would certainly be fatal.

For two days we prayed. Then we cautiously removed the pack, checking her heart rate all the time for the first sign of haemorrhage. The pulse remained steady. Next day its beat continued regular and strong. She never looked back. We asked, 'Why, after all God's amazing help to her, does she not turn at once to him in gratitude and faith?'

God's timetable is different from ours. Akiduri was carrying an early pregnancy. Only a Turkana foetus could have survived that enormous trauma and loss of blood. Seven months later she gave birth and called the babe 'Daktari' in an expression of a gratitude we had not seen before. She became a firm friend, obtained work in the home of our missionary nurses and eventually joined the church.

God sent us precious workers. A mechanic and his wife lifted the burden of building and maintenance and helped enormously in the church ministries. Two nurses and a hospital administrator transformed the hospital into a clean, efficient unit and assisted with the developing safari programme. While longing to ease the immense suffering which we saw all round us, we shared a conviction that the ultimate answer lay in the transforming power of the gospel. Daily we met to beseech God to bless our Lokori neighbours and the 200,000 people throughout the tribe. In the fellowship of committed hearts we became what one preacher has called 'a community of possibility'. I had read Isaiah's longing for a blaze of blessing as a plaintive groan; now it became a positive goal.

Ezekiel worked as driver for the DC and lived in Lodwar. He told us, 'As a young man I was trained as a boxer and often travelled long distances for tournaments, even as far as Congo. I won many cups and earned much money, but found no satisfaction because my life was full of sin. I used to buy beer by the crate and forced my attention on many girls. My heart was full of pride and I despised other people. Especially I hated a pastor who visited my home and I threatened to hurl burning coals at him if he persisted. But the Lord spoke to me and led me to turn from my sin and receive Jesus as Saviour.'

Ezekiel married a lovely Christian girl who had grown up in Lokori school and then worked for us in the hospital. His job frequently took him away from home, while the burden of caring for small children, often sick, rested mainly on her.

Ever present relatives and friends whispered that her husband was unfaithful to her: 'You had better consult the witch doctor,' they advised. Pressures multiplied and became too heavy for her mind. She was brought to our home, raving and blaspheming. Our team prayed for a week and she recovered – a stronger Christian and a more trusting wife than before – and became a church leader in Lodwar.

*****

Our pilot Gordon contacted me. He said, 'In MAF we've been glad to help you with emergency flying, but we'd love to do more. We want to be at the cutting edge of evangelism. Is there any way we can help in Turkana?' I replied, 'Gordon, how could we ever afford to use a plane?'

We decided to attempt a preliminary flight and a Christian farmer, who worshipped with Gordon at Nairobi Baptist Church, heard Gordon praying about this need and offered to finance the first trip. I prepared four airstrips in South Turkana and we visited them in a small Cessna – preaching and treating the sick. When Gordon reported back to his church, the congregation decided to pay for a second, more extensive safari. We dreamt of a regular programme and asked God for the money. A Nairobi-based famine relief committee became interested and helped us for many months. When this source finished God provided another.

When I was in Nairobi on business I received a call from the German Embassy, 'Will you please visit the Ambassador's wife to discuss eye disease among the Turkana.' As we sat on her verandah sipping tea, she told us about her concern for preventing blindness and she enquired, 'Do you treat much eye disease?' I told her about the desert wind which drives sand into thousands of eyes; well-meaning friends dig out the offending grit with a thorn and leave a blinding scar on the cornea. I explained that an operation could sometimes restore sight. She seemed interested so I went on to talk about a tribe we visited by plane to the south where everyone suffered from running eyes and some became blind as a result. Flies fed on the infected fluid and carried it from face to face. 'Wash your faces each morning,' I instructed them, 'and you will discourage the flies.' 'But we love flies,' they responded. 'They always buzz around our cattle. Our wealth is in cattle. Flies are a sign that we have many cows.' When the infection becomes chronic the eyelid scars and turns inwards so that lashes scrape the front of the eye and ruin its surface. Simple eyelid surgery can bring enormous relief and save sight. To prevent blindness we wanted to visit often, to teach, to provide medicine and simple surgery. The aristocratic lady listened and I thought she might find a few tubes of eye ointment for us. How greatly I underestimated her kind influence!

A few weeks later two letters arrived from Christian organisations in Germany. The Christoffel Blindenmission enquired if we needed help with travel, medicines, optical instruments or hospital fees for eye patients. The letter concluded with the warning that we need not apply for assistance towards buildings: 'We do not believe in Christian cement.' The other group, Bread for the World, wondered if we had any capital needs towards our hospital structures. Over many years both these organisations gave generously, enabling us to enlarge our ministry to the blind and to people threatened with loss of sight.

We developed a rota for visiting a string of outlying centres regularly, running clinics, and often sheltered only by a canvas sheet over the wing of the plane. We preached, visited homes and flew seriously ill people to Lokori. Next we placed a teacher and a Lokori-trained nurse at several of these places, encouraging them to share their faith. Pastor Peter joined us as we visited them every few weeks and slowly churches began to form. Loneliness and lawlessness tested the Christian commitment of these pioneers to the limit, but a team of witnesses grew across Turkana.

*****

Hostile tribes surrounded Turkana. Bands of warriors invaded border areas, killing people and stealing their cattle. Active men fled, leaving women and children to suffer the brunt of the attack. A few months later the Turkana mounted a revenge attack and the tragedy was repeated, this time in the homes of their enemies. A cycle of murder was set up, leaving us with the ugly task of tending the wounded. At first we treated a few spear wounds but, after Idi Amin's violent reign in Uganda in the seventies, the whole area became awash with automatic weapons and deaths escalated into more than a hundred on an average raid, with few survivors. As the warrior bands swept through a swathe of country, all the Turkana moved away for a time, and we had to withdraw our African colleagues, leaving bandits to plunder our simple buildings and, worse, Satan to rob a community of the first glimmers of faith.

Famine continued to ravage the country from time to time. I often remembered the garden areas downstream where the people had initially been hostile. The river flow was so uncertain that they could never depend upon crops. We wondered, 'Could we control this flow into a more dependable source of water for irrigation?' When we took some silt to a Nairobi laboratory for testing, they told us that the soil was rich. We invited experts from TEAR Fund and Nairobi University to advise on the digging of ditches, the control of water from the river and the choice of the best crops. Missionary agriculturalists joined our team. Thanks to the school system they could now employ workers with at least a primary education, and a few were Christians. Some tribal leaders grumbled because we failed to introduce diesel-operated pumps, but we wanted a simple, hand-controlled system which local people could own and operate without depending on fuel, spare parts or mechanics from outside Turkana. Hundreds settled around these fields, growing their own food and listening to the message of Christ. Several new churches developed.

For that message to lodge in minds and hearts, the Turkana needed to read it for themselves. By 1975 Joan's committee had worked through about two-thirds of the New Testament. We estimated that Joan and her team of translators might finish it in another two years. After eighteen years the Lord had won the battle to get established: hospitals at Lokori and Kalokol were saving lives; our team was delivering a rudimentary health care system through much of Turkana; hundreds of youngsters attended our schools; God had carved out eighteen churches and seemed to be selecting some leaders for them. If life hummed along too busily sometimes, at least we usually felt able to cope.

In many ways – health care, agriculture, Bible translation and education; by love, patience, zeal and preaching; by introducing people to the Lord Jesus and planting new churches across our wide parish – God was alleviating Turkana distress and feeding fuel to the fire of his own purposes. Some Turkana, in blunt kindness, said to us, *'Tomojong kane'* (Grow old here) and others, *'Toton nege'* (Die here). We saw a multitude of challenges and would gladly have agreed to their invitation to spend the rest of our years with them, but the question began to niggle. Will that be best for the church? Are they not even now a little too dependent on us? Is God calling others, more able than us, to take these young churches forward? Does he have work for us elsewhere?

But where? I recalled something Pastor Peter said in response to a church elder who insisted that he continue a fruitful ministry which he had pursued among them for ten years, 'God called me to follow Paul's guidance, "It has always been my ambition to preach the Gospel where Christ is not known"' (Rom. 15:20). While we recognised that God calls many in a different direction, Joan and I believed that he wanted us to share the same ambition. Our thoughts fluctuated between a Muslim tribe in north-eastern Kenya and a neglected island in the Indian Ocean. God did not permit Joan to finish the translation (he had a better plan for that); suddenly he pulled us right out of Turkana into a totally different sphere.

*****

In 1974 some AIM leaders who had attended the Lausanne Congress on Evangelism challenged the Mission's governing body, the International Council, with their enthusiastic report. With a shock, council members realised that 'more than two thirds of the world have yet to be evangelised ... this is the time to pray earnestly for the salvation of the unreached and to launch new efforts to achieve world evangelisation'

(Lausanne Covenant, 1974, Clause 9). They asked, 'What about our part of Africa?' The delegates began to list neglected groups of people, tribes, even whole nations: many in the northern and coastal parts of Kenya, in vast sections of Tanzania and Sudan, the Comoro and Seychelle Islands in the Indian Ocean, and Mozambique....; the possibilities seemed endless.

They decided to appoint an Associate Secretary for Outreach to investigate, encourage and implement outreach into such new areas. Sitting among the delegates, I found my heart warming to the discussion for it seemed that we were underlining the principle reason for which God had called our society into existence eighty years earlier. I gave little thought to the practical implications to the individual who would take on this mammoth task – that he and his wife might need to pay a price in terms of their present ministry, family, home, comfort and security – until a finger pointed at us. The Chairman drew me aside and said, 'Several of the senior men here feel you and Joan should accept this responsibility.' Bearing in mind the steady spread of work across Turkana, he added, 'What we now want is not just addition, but multiplication.'

We did not find it easy to leave our many friends and home in Turkana. For Joan it meant handing the translation over to others and saying farewell to a programme of women's meetings, visiting and choir training (she had found the people loved music and quickly started producing their own hymns). On my part, I wondered how the church work and health care would continue after our departure. We asked ourselves too, how will God use Joan's musical and linguistic skills and my own experience in evangelism, pastoring, medicine and surgery? And what had we taken on? Could we possibly fulfil the expectations of our leaders? Michael Green's words at Lausanne challenged me, 'It would seem to me that the church today, throughout the West at any rate, is paralysed by a crippling lack of mobility. Is there not, I wonder, a growing materialism that saps our total dedication to Christ and willingness to go anywhere and do anything if the Spirit should so lead?' Although materialism had never worried us, we did recognise the danger of becoming so settled in some success that we missed God's mandate to move on.

Our three youngsters took the change in their stride. Mary, just turned sixteen, Helen, at fourteen, and Donald, sixteen months younger, relished the idea of a home in Nairobi. Their thrice yearly trips to the Kenyan highlands had given way to secondary schools in England. For teenagers, Nairobi posed much more attractive holiday possibilities than remote Lokori – friends from school days in Kenya, swimming pools, access to the coast with its sandy beaches. But they had maturer concerns too. When we discussed the move they said, 'If that's God's will, it's what we want.'

On August 28th a wealthy African friend in Nairobi sent up a plane to move Joan's precious piano. At 1 am next morning the moon shone kindly on Donald and me as we set off on the long drive south. Unusual rain had softened the desert's harsh face with long grass which waved in a gentle breeze as we crept across familiar dry river beds for the last time. In the afternoon we watched for a little Cessna above us flying Joan and the girls to Nairobi. We all met in the city and, four days later, I drove them to the airport for the flight to London, where Joan was planning to settle Donald into Tonbridge School, Kent, while the girls resumed their studies in Wadhurst. The final hugs came quickly. With a familiar sinking feeling, I watched them disappear past the immigration desks, and then returned to an empty flat, as yet almost bare of furniture.

At last the flickering flames were burning steadily in the young Turkana churches but our own task there was accomplished. I felt God turning the clock back eighteen years to a new beginning, as fraught with uncertainty and difficulty as it had been then.

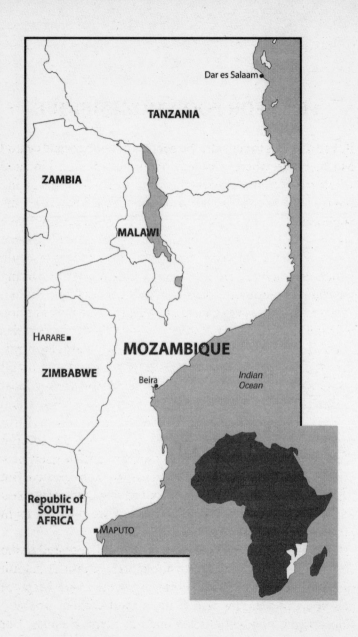

7

PRAY FOR POOR MOZAMBIQUE

IC had asked us to consider the peoples of northern and central Mozambique where a veneer of formal religion hindered whole tribes from experiencing Jesus Christ as a life-giving Saviour and friend. On my own now for a few weeks, the euphoria of changing to a new and challenging task gave way to perplexity. In the month we moved from Turkana, Mozambique celebrated independence from Portuguese rule which had endured for almost five hundred years. During that time, according to the first President, Samora Machel, 'The cross and the sword were identified as being in collusion with the hierarchy of the Roman Catholic Church.' Centuries of colonial prejudice greatly hindered the work of Protestants, then seven years of civil war closed the country to almost all missionaries. In 1974 the colonists permitted a transitional Government, part Portuguese and part Mozambican, and doors swung open. Surely now, I reasoned, a fully independent country would allow freedom for foreign Christians to serve the existing churches and to plant new congregations in the spiritual wastes where none existed. But I asked myself, 'How do you take the first steps when you know no-one there and cannot speak a word of the main language, Portuguese?'

The obvious answer seemed, 'Go!' So I enquired at the British High Commission in Nairobi about a visa. A helpful official assured me, 'Fly to Lourenço Marques (now Maputo) and you can obtain a visa at the airport without trouble.' Encouraged, I bought a ticket and travellers' cheques. But next day, the Deputy High Commissioner rang to say, 'I've been in touch with Lourenco Marques and on no account may you enter without a visa. Send a telegram.' A week later he cautioned patience, 'It will take time.' When no answer came from Mozambique I decided to try in Dar-es-Salaam, because Tanzania had hosted the Mozambican political leaders and freedom fighters during their long years of exile. Perhaps I would find an official there who could authorise my entry.

A week in Dar failed to produce a visa, but I met some interesting people. Mr Nusch, the leader of fifty workers of the Christian Mission to Many Lands (CMML) mostly located along the Tanzania-Mozambique border, spoke of meeting thousands of Mozambican refugees and soldiers. FRELIMO (The Front for the Liberation of Mozambique) mounted raids against the Portuguese from big camps north of the border. Opportunities for ministry abounded and many responded. Nusch talked of the joy of seeing a Christian soldier setting off with his pockets full of Scriptures and tracts to distribute to his fellow Mozambicans. But he warned me, 'FRELIMO is martial' and told me of several difficult encounters with soldiers, some not yet in their teens. One night gun-toting men in uniform stopped his car. They commanded, 'Turn off the lights and get out.... One person come forward.' So Nusch advanced with an official letter which authorised him to travel in the area. The soldier, keeping his finger on the trigger of an automatic rifle pointing at Nusch, reached out his other hand for the letter and appeared to read it with the help of a torch under his armpit. The hand shook so much that the letter fell. Nusch noticed the man looking at his empty left hand as if still reading. Then he realised the soldier, holding the barrel of his gun a few inches from Nusch's chest, could read nothing for he was hopelessly drunk.

To my question, 'Do you think I could get into Mozambique across the northern border?' he simply shook his head. Other Christians in Dar confirmed his negative assessment. I located a small FRELIMO office in Dar, but the clerks told me that all the important people had moved back home. They said, 'We're all going now that FRELIMO is in power.'

The inland border of Mozambique runs for 2,500 miles, along the edges of Tanzania, Malawi, Zambia, Zimbabwe, South Africa and Swaziland. If access was not possible from Kenya or Tanzania, maybe I should explore further south. I spent a day in Malawi as a guest of Africa Evangelical Fellowship. The leader of their missionary team had received an invitation from local FRELIMO commanders to minister within Mozambique, but he was wary, 'We view this with caution. A hard, anti-missionary feeling in the heart of the new government has not yet reached the periphery.' Entry by that route might result in an initial welcome, but it could turn disastrously sour. I continued my journey to South Africa.

As soon as I arrived in Johannesburg I met abundant evidence of FRELIMO's hard attitude. The Manager of a Christian bookshop who had been in Lorenço Marques told me, 'The Government commanded me to sell my present stock and then leave. Meanwhile they froze my bank account.' The regime jailed a young man who was ministering to drug addicts. Pastor Doll of the Nazarene Church, returning to Mozambique, was arrested at the border with two colleagues and held in solitary confinement. I met a Pastor Eduardo who told me that he planned to go back immediately to the Mozambican capital because twenty-six fellow pastors were in prison, leaving their churches leaderless. The government had already closed many churches and Bible Schools, confiscating much property. It forbade evangelism outside church buildings, and made it illegal to influence a child under eighteen – even a baby bound to its mother's back – by bringing them into a church service. The President proudly announced, 'We are the first truly Marxist Government in Africa' and adopted as motto, *A lutta continua* (The struggle continues).

Back in Nairobi, Bishop Mulwa, the leader of the Africa Inland Church Kenya (AICK), invited me to tell the Central Church Council about my trip. The African leaders warmed to the challenge. I suggested an approach to the Government by Africans. Bishop Mulwa was keen to go, but we decided to invite the Tanzanian Bishop (of AICT) to join the party because of the cordial relationship between his country and Mozambique. Months later the Tanzanian replied, 'I discussed it with my Council and we decided we have so much to do here we cannot get involved.' And there the matter rested. Meanwhile many more Christians began to pray earnestly for Mozambique.

*****

For seven years we prayed for Mozambique. At our Nairobi home all the news we received spoke of mounting Marxist oppression, a tattered economy and poverty-stricken people. But, unknown to us, God was answering our cries to him and working miracles in the most unlikely situations: some through dreams; others by healing in answer to prayer; more, directly through the Word of God.

Years earlier a teenager obtained a copy of John's Gospel and read it several times. Convinced of the truth of Jesus, he ceased to venerate the ancestral spirits of his Sena Tribe. Family hostility forced him to leave home and he found his way into Southern Rhodesia (now Zimbabwe) where he linked up with an independent church. He developed a great love for the Word of God, reading it constantly and often discussing it. The church leader baptised him and encouraged him to evangelise. With an open Bible in his hands, he wandered back into his own country and found that his fellow Sena people knew nothing of this liberating message. Many listened, believed and banded into little churches.

In the late sixties FRELIMO began their seven year rebellion against the colonists. The Portuguese conscripted the young evangelist into their army but, when he refused to fight against his own countrymen, put him in jail. As a prisoner, with time on his hands, he studied the Bible by Emmaus Correspondence Course, and continued studying after his release. His Bishop surprised him by demanding that he abandon this programme and, when he refused, dismissed him. The churches he had founded continued to look to him for leadership, insisting that he establish them into a new denomination: *Igreja Nova Allianca* (The New Covenant Church).

Churches multiplied and other leaders sprang up, some lacking his commitment to the Bible. A few became jealous and, when the Marxist government came to power, saw their chance to oust this zealous preacher by accusing him. Once more he found himself in prison, forced into hard labour. But God was with him. The authorities arranged a People's Trial. They shut him inside a cage on the back of a lorry and drove him into the midst of a crowd. Although the charges made little sense, the multitude obediently declared him guilty but, before they could pronounce the inevitable sentence to death, the skies opened and an immense downpour forced every one to flee. Soaked to the skin, they drove him back to prison where, four months later, they released him – as he believed, in answer to prayer.

Marxism failed Mozambique. An increasingly popular resistance movement created havoc in many parts of the country, effectively cutting railways, closing roads and occasionally plunging the second city, Beira, into darkness by severing power lines. In Maputo a bank clerk suddenly found himself the manager. Anyone efficiently running a factory, a sugar plantation or even a small market garden, could face a charge of 'Capitalist' before the local People's Cell. So factories closed, farming ceased, banks collapsed and prisons filled. Only the army and police prospered, trained and armed by Russia, which was recompensed by the right to maintain a large fishing fleet off the coast.

In December 1982, President Machel, realising that his oppression of the churches had alienated a potentially supportive segment of his people, called a workshop of religious leaders, including the Sena evangelist. Machel told them, 'We want to make real the principles of religious liberty and the fact of a secular state.' In reaction against the monolithic form of Catholicism imposed by the Portuguese he went on, 'Before anything else our churches must be Mozambican. They must not represent churches outside the country.' He appealed to the leaders to help with development and to foster unity. A small group of church leaders prepared a written response agreeing with his requests but requesting also, 'visits by missionaries ... and invitations to theological teachers with a view to temporary ministry in Bible schools and seminaries.' They explained that, without such aid, they could never develop able indigenous leaders.

The co-ordinator of the Emmaus Courses, Arthur, wrote to me from his home in Harare, Zimbabwe, to say that his ex-pupil wanted to sponsor missionaries willing to assist the churches along these lines. I sent a letter to the evangelist, asking him to try for a visa. It seemed like a miracle when he posted the precious document; even more so when, in late August, Arthur and I stopped at Customs and Immigration on the Zimbabwe/Mozambique border, lent the official a cheap biro so that he could sign our documents, and drove at last into a devastated land.

I could hardly believe we had made it so easily. Back in Nairobi that border post had seemed like an impregnable fortress barring all entry. But now it was behind us, and we could speed along a tarmac road eastwards across the waist of Mozambique. At frequent checkpoints soldiers searched our car and then asked for cigarettes. I learnt to say, '*Eo nao fumo*' (I don't smoke), and we proffered tracts instead. Three gutted railway carriages grimly reminded us of the senseless loss of life in the hit-and-run tactics of the 'Resistance'. We skirted a bridge damaged in a bomb blast and, at a wider river outside Beira, trundled across pontoons replacing a viaduct blasted to pieces a few months before. We met the evangelist at the entrance to a block of flats and he led us up to the home of a hospitable teacher and his wife. They possessed little but shared it generously.

City life, when an economy collapses, presents many anomalies. Our host boasted a modern flushing toilet, but it depended on a rubber diaphragm which had long since perished. Other little gadgets – like a door handle, a window latch, a tap, a light bulb or its switch – break and cannot be replaced. The lift collapses – tough when you live on the seventh floor. A few elderly cars run in the streets, their tyres worn to the canvas and batteries so difficult to replace that a wise driver only switches on his lights at night when he sees another vehicle approaching. To obtain bread you rise before dawn, join a queue at the bakery and stand for several hours, often to be disappointed. We saw no milk during our fortnight there. Shops contained almost nothing; people joked, 'If you see a queue anywhere, join it first and then find out why.'

Every evening we preached; first the evangelist in Chisena, then Arthur in Portuguese which the pastor translated, and finally me in English with double interpretation. I had never met Christians so eager to hear teaching.

A threatening police presence sat like a cloud over the whole of life. Driving home after a wonderful meeting, smart men, clad in khaki and armed with ominous revolvers, waved us down. I could feel the fear that gripped our group of Christians as they fumbled for their documents, for they knew that the police were searching for unemployed people to send to distant labour camps.

Our friend introduced us to many churches, both of his own denomination and others. They had sprung up during the troubled days of war. But he still grieved over whole tribes which still lacked a vibrant message of the Lord Jesus Christ. He told me, 'I am an evangelist, not a pastor; I long to go north to the many unreached people but I cannot desert these new churches. Why don't you come and teach the Christians and release me to follow my calling?' He took us south to Maputo to introduce us to officials in the Department for Religious Affairs in the Ministry of Justice, who requested a letter explaining all we wished to do. My friends showed me how to write and kindly translated into a flowery Portuguese: 'I respectfully come in this manner to solicit from your excellency the favour of accepting this letter in which I set out the reason for my presence at this time on the soil of the People's Republic of Mozambique ...' and so on for several paragraphs and then, 'I would like to suggest that our organisation send workers to help develop further the programme for training church leaders for the *Igreja Nova Allianca* ... and other churches.' I told him we wanted the churches to possess the programme from the beginning and eventually run it without outside aid. The evangelist agreed to follow up our application, saying, 'Don't worry if you hear no more. The test of their acceptance will be your next application for a visa.'

*****

Seven months later I flew to Harare again, this time with Joan. I tried to hide my sense of anxiety from her. Government had indeed given us a visa but for the wrong date (a month previously) and for the wrong place of entry (Maputo instead of Beira). We had been able to arrange no vehicle for the journey, no interpreter, no place to stay in Beira, no schedule of contacts either with church or government leaders. Worst of all I was planning to take my wife along a road often subject to guerilla attack. Was I crazy? When I awoke next morning in our friend's Harare home, a morbid cloud of fear oppressed me. Sitting up in her bed Joan said, 'I'm reading each day in Exodus. Listen to today's portion.' And she read from chapter 23, 'See, I am sending an angel ahead of you to guard you along the way and to bring you to the place I have prepared. Pay attention to him and listen to what he says ... If you listen carefully to what he says and do all that I say, I will be an enemy to your enemies....' My depression lifted. That day a Christian lent us a red Peugeot 506 (it ran on diesel – our angel knew that Beira pumps stocked this fuel but almost no petrol); we met a Mozambican Bible School student, who needed to travel to Beira and would interpret for us for our fortnight there; and the Mozambique Embassy in Harare graciously attended to all our visa problems in record time. We packed the car with food and Scriptures and set off.

We paused briefly to look up a church leader at a place called Nhamatanda. While drinking his wife's tea, we heard a scuffle behind the house, wings flapping and a chicken squawking. Joan's glance at me spoke louder than words, 'That's lunch! You can forget about going on quickly.' We enjoyed fellowship and our host promised to meet us next day in the city with a few church leaders to decide who we needed to contact. As we pulled away in the Peugeot, we saw soldiers leading a group of boys and young men with no shirts or shoes. The student explained, 'They've grabbed them for the army and taken their clothes to prevent them running away.' We passed a cement factory and read the proud slogan at the entrance, 'Workers of the world unite.' But no workers passed those gates; they had been shut for many months.

A Goan/Mozambican brother and sister arranged a comfortable flat for us and gave us all sorts of helpful advice. They told us, 'You may have only a year or two until the Government once again expels missionaries.' The next day, Sunday, provided several preaching opportunities in preparation for Easter week. For two weeks we crisscrossed the city, meeting church people of many denominations, both of us sharing in ministry and all the time asking God to show us his plan for AIM in Mozambique.

Most services consisted of rollicking hymns with much clapping and swaying. While I was preaching about the resurrection on Easter Day, a little dance in the aisle interrupted my flow. The people hungered for Bible teaching and quietened into attentive silence when we opened our Bibles. Sometimes, when we finished and sat down, the leader would enquire, 'Do you have any more teaching for us?' and I would start again. Most services ended with sick people kneeling at the front for prayer. Collection time always impressed us as worshippers, clad in the poorest of clothes, danced with joy to the front, placing their gifts on the table. Afterwards the leader usually collected the cash and handed it to us, 'for fuel for your car.' They thanked us for coming and begged, 'Tell your friends to pray for poor Mozambique.'

On our last day our evangelist friend arrived from Maputo and chatted to us in the teacher's flat. We told him, 'We think AIM would like to send Bible teachers who would preach in churches (when asked) and train Bible teachers, evangelists and Mozambican cross-cultural missionaries. Starting in Beira, we would hope to move out to other centres as the Lord establishes new churches.'

*****

Eighteen months later the first AIM team was ready to enter Mozambique. Don Potocki, a bachelor pilot working for AIM-AIR, responded to God's clear call, abandoning his flying profession in East Africa to become a full-time preacher in Mozambique. Through a misunderstanding at Nairobi airport he had Kenyan money in his pocket and only narrowly escaped arrest by customs officers. In Harare he telephoned his mother in America to say farewell. She told him that his father's liver cancer was advancing and might soon take his life. Immediately he was torn between two responsibilities: should he continue to Mozambique or fly to his family. After a difficult time of prayer he decided to go to Beira.

Family considerations threatened to hinder Randy Fennig. Following a year of language study in Portugal with his wife, Toni, and two children, we timed his arrival in Harare to coincide with ours. He joined us from Johannesburg in a second-hand Volkswagen, expecting his family to arrive later. But conditions in Mozambique forced him to question the rightness of taking his family there. Should he turn back at this last step? To my immense relief he decided to go forward, and I was able to settle these two men in Beira and introduce them to church leaders. When I returned to Zimbabwe two weeks later, I phoned Toni in Portugal confirming arrangements for Randy to meet her and the children in Harare.

God called others to join our team so that fifteen years later thirty-five AIM missionaries served different churches, co-operating with workers from other organisations. More are now preparing to go. Our own responsibilities multiplied elsewhere and we reluctantly took our hands off a ministry whose birth had challenged us over ten years. Progress had varied: often static, occasionally speedy, sometimes moving off in the wrong direction – but eventually reaching our goal. Our last departure from the seventh floor flat of Meque's friend epitomised our experience. The lift shot down to the ground floor but declined to open its gate, whisking us instead to the tenth floor. Finally it compromised, permitting us to exit on the second floor and then descend by the stairs.

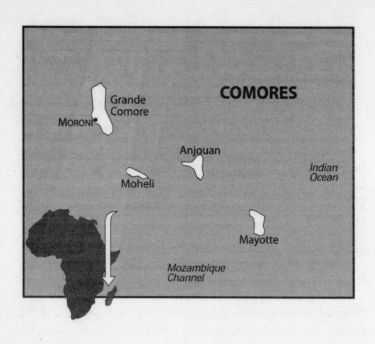

8

TIDES CHANGE IN THE
COMORO ISLANDS

In the mid-seventies Africans, breathing the heady air of independence, changed systems and overturned governments, unleashing powerful currents which swept aside ancient barriers to the gospel. Shakespeare wrote, 'There is a tide in the affairs of men, which, taken at the flood, leads on to fortune.' Our task was to recognise that high-tide when God wanted us to launch our frail barque on to the turbulent waters.

In August 1975, at the same time as Samora Machel came to power in Mozambique, another independence drama was swiftly developing among the Comoro Islands in the Indian Ocean, two hundred miles to the east. Unlike the Mozambican revolutionaries who fought the colonial power for seven years before obtaining their goal, the Comorian *Mapinduzi* (Overturners) no sooner threatened to fight for their freedom than their French masters replied, 'You can have it!' As if glad to be rid of a costly burden, France began to recall their 140 secondary school teachers, a mass of health care professionals, engineers, air traffic controllers, etc., and to freeze all payments.

Just before independence, AIM leaders, sensing a turn of tide in this Islamic country, had explored the possibility of sharing the gospel with these people for the first time. Several paid brief visits and then a seasoned American couple, Hal and Sally Olsen, and a new South African, Miriam van Reenen, rented a bungalow at the north end of Grande

Comore, made some friends and began to learn the language. The Olsens left after six weeks and a Canadian, Millie Coulton, joined Miriam. When the Mapinduzi seemed set for violence, the Mission withdrew the two ladies.

*****

By November Joan had come home to Nairobi from England and we began thinking about the Comoro Islands. Millie felt mystified, 'What is the point of returning so soon?' Political unrest had forced her to leave and we respected her real concern for our safety, but we wondered, 'Could the resulting chaos create just the opportunity we need? Will social change shake closed minds so that they open to new truth?' We asked God for guidance and decided, yes, this could be God's time.

A kind missionary friend drove us to Nairobi Airport. Familiar with management principles, he enquired, 'Dick, what are your goals for this safari?' Uncertainties and anxieties churned in my mind as I fumbled for words, 'Well David.... We've heard of one Christian in the Comoros. We plan to meet him and see what develops.'

Two hundred miles off the east coast of Africa we saw a volcano dramatically rearing its head 7,750 feet into the clouds. We could understand the early Arab navigators who, observing horizontal strips of cloud climbing towards a hidden peak, got the impression of a ladder and named the island, '*Ngazi idja*' (the ladder is coming). Drawing nearer we could see the mountainside green with trees but gashed brown where the crater, five miles wide, had sent streams of fiery magma down to the ocean. One of these had flowed close to the capital in the distant past giving its name, *Moroni* (The Hot Place).

A broad smile at the airport showed us our Christian and

he escorted us to the home of the Assistant Airport Manager whose pretty wife prepared tea and brought her little daughter for Joan to hug. The Assistant Manager then settled us into his blue Peugeot. Realising that I winced at a recurring grumble from the gearbox, he explained the state of machinery on the island with a story about his friend's bicycle. 'He was cycling at night when a policeman commanded him to stop because he carried no light. "I can't stop!" he yelled back; "I've got no brakes!"' The Manager continued, 'As long as the car runs, we don't worry about a few rumbles.'

We sped northwards around a small harbour, through narrow streets lined by old Arab-type houses with minarets of mosques spiking up here and there above the huddled roofs. Our host pointed out a new parliament building on the left but explained, 'No-one meets there yet.' When I asked who was governing the country, he replied, 'We don't know.' I enquired if he had been in danger during the revolution. 'Well no,' he answered, 'we are peaceable people. When the *Mapinduzi* threatened trouble, some folk asked what the noise was about and then went on playing football.'

I enquired, 'What was it all about?'

The two friends launched into a long history of occupation by Arab settlers followed by Portuguese and finally French. Over a century of colonial rule convinced France that these islands could not profit the motherland and she therefore promised to hand over to a Comorian government eventually. Officials groomed Comorian counterparts, even allowing the people to elect a national President to shadow the French Governor. My friends finished, 'They refused to hand over the power, so our leaders decided to take it.'

Our road took us twenty-five miles, half the length of the island, along a black lava-strewn coast where the clear lapping

101

sea changed from emerald to turquoise and a deep azure blue. To our right a forest of coconuts scaled the volcano. Banana plantations cradled poor villages, mostly constructed from palm fronds with an occasional stone building and always several mosques. Finally we ran alongside a mile of beach to a small, unfinished house furnished with two wooden-framed beds having rope for springs and straw bags for mattresses. Joan's kitchen consisted of a one-ringed oil stove in the corner – the only other piece of furniture.

Our host told us his story.

A South African Christian, Chris Fourrie, desired to assist needy people in the islands of the Indian Ocean and, requiring an English speaking contact, was given the name of our friend. He arrived by air, came north to one of the two modern hotels on the island and asked the bus driver if he knew this man. He answered, 'Oh yes. He's my brother-in-law!' Each day the young man chatted with Chris. The South African told him about his concern for the poor, enquiring about development needs in the islands and what he could do to help from his own country. They talked too about the *Injil* (gospel) – a term familiar to the Comorian who had been reared on the Koran. Chris's discussion of sin and salvation through Christ mystified him at first but, by the end of ten days, he began to think there might be something in it all. Later he wrote to Chris in South Africa, 'Do you remember that book you told me about? Please send me a copy.' Chris sent *Good News for Modern Man*. The book fascinated him as he read it from start to finish. He turned back to Matthew chapter one and went through it again. Intrigued, he pored over the pages for a third time. After seven journeys through the book he knew the Lord Jesus as his Saviour.

We wandered around the small town, surprised to find

many who simply wished to talk. Mohammed, in a long white robe and green waistcoat and speaking perfect Swahili, told us of his time as a barman in an elite Nairobi bar in the era of the Mau Mau rebellion. 'They wanted a Muslim because I didn't drink,' he explained. 'And, when the rebels attacked looking for money, they took me out to the forest and beat me up because I refused to hand over the contents of the till.' When Jacques, one of a hundred children born to a virile Frenchman, said he had been fishing all night and caught nothing, we told him about Peter's experience, 'How about following Jesus and learning to catch men?' A bespectacled elder, Salah, produced two coconuts, deftly swung his sharp machete to cut an inch-wide drinking hole in each, handed them to us and then, when we had drunk the refreshing cool milk, sliced them in half, fashioning a spoon from the outside so that we could gouge out the nutritious pearly-white lining. Another barman talked about his brother, a captain in the Zanzibar Army, who had assassinated the Prime Minister and then taken his own life.

As we sauntered along the beach we saw some small motor boats, gifts to fishermen following Chris' enquiries about development. Several friendly old men knew Millie and Miriam and had met others of our Mission. They wanted to talk about aid, and begged us to help with staff and supplies for the hospital and clinics, as well as teachers to replace the departing French. Then our Christian said, 'Tell them about the two sons.' Mohammed in the green jacket interpreted as I recounted the story of the prodigal and his self-righteous brother. Little pillbox hats, decorated with skilfully-embroidered Koranic verses, nodded as this powerful story struck home for the first time.

We walked through coastal villages and clambered up to

others perched on the side of the mountain. News of our activities must have spread, for two dignified men called on us to ask why we had come. They announced, 'The Minister for Defence wishes to meet you and we will set up an appointment in the next day or two.' Fearful lest he think we were French spies, we comforted ourselves with the knowledge that he would soon change his mind when he heard us attempt one sentence in French.

When the time came, we called on a mansion sitting on a seaside cliff, and sank into deep armchairs in a room tastefully decorated in green and gold. While we waited, my friend gave me some of the Minister's biography. Ali Soilih, returning from Paris with a degree in agriculture, was made Director of the Comorian Agricultural Society. Funds disappeared and the shadow President dismissed him. When the President died (by poison, according to some), his successor, Abdallah, gave Soilih the post of Minister of Works, but sacked him after some disagreement. In a virtually bloodless coup of August 4th he gained control of the country.

A beautifully carved door swung open, we stood and the Minister swept in. He motioned us to sit facing him, a weary man with a round face and bulging eyes. In answer to his question I explained the Mission's activities on the mainland of Africa – health care, education, literacy, translation, literature preparation, agriculture – trying to meet the needs of people wherever we meet them. 'Most of all,' I concluded, 'We like to share our faith with people who want to hear.'

I thought, 'Now I've blown it!' But his next words were like balm. 'We need help; and we will accept it from anywhere we can find it.' With that encouragement I visited the main hospital where a Dr Tourqui presented a catalogue of personnel needs. The Director of UNICEF underlined the top priority, 'Find a surgeon. By this one move you will resolve 90% of your problems in gaining acceptance for your organisation.'

Our return to Kenya coincided with the annual conference of our three hundred missionaries. The Executive Officer generously invited me to share the sadness of visiting a nation with only one Christian, and the joy of finding many opportunities for pioneer ministry. I asked them, 'Would some of you uproot, at least temporarily, and face this challenge?' As a result I was able to make a quick trip to Moroni on Boxing Day and offer Dr Tourqui and the UNICEF leader (who told me he was now Director of Medical Services) two surgeons in succession, a laboratory technician, a nurse/ midwife, an engineer and my own services part-time. On their side they promised four houses, two little Renault cars and four return air fares. By January 17th 1976 we stood on the Airport tarmac to greet our new team.

*****

Rain poured down as Joan and I settled inside our hospital home. Rats scampered over a bin of uncollected garbage in the back yard. Mosquitoes swarmed: one type flew by day injecting filaria (which causes elephantiasis) and another buzzed at night carrying a deadly cargo of malaria. Dr Tourqui added me to his surgical team, assigning me to the maternity ward with Sheila Jones as Sister in charge. But a Comorian Sister, the divorced wife of the Minister of Health, maintained her own control and we tried to live with the resulting tension. Patient care rested in the hands of relatives, who thronged the wards and slept on the verandahs. They threw on to the ground the remnants of bananas, mangoes, paw paws, pineapples and oranges which provided meals for the patients, as well as feeding an army of rodents and an air force of flies. The few rubbish bins overflowed with old dressings. I appealed to the Hospital Superintendent, 'You talk about *Mapinduzi*; what about a revolution in hygiene?' He responded to our appeal by expelling relatives and placing a guard on the gates to permit them in only at visiting times. But we achieved less in our attempts to improve standards in clinical care. Madame in maternity flouted my instructions, frequently treating my patients with powerful medicines I had not prescribed, and Sheila's position became increasingly difficult.

Frustration dogged the steps of each team member and several spoke of return to the controllable conditions of Kenya. Each evening we walked out to one of the team homes on The Hill of Lava to pray. But for that fellowship I don't think any of us would have survived. On a low day in February Haggai spoke to our hearts, 'Be strong and work for I am with you.... Take courage;' and we praised God for the priceless privilege of demonstrating his love. With the arrival of two teachers and a dentist, our numbers swelled to eleven.

The government offered us well-built houses which had been vacated by the French. But filth reigned. Joan, Sheila and Frances paused in a lengthy cleanup to recollect that they had each studied at different times at Redcliffe Missionary College in London, where, among more biblical subjects, the teachers insisted that they learn how to clean toilets. Then, it had seemed so unnecessary. Now, they chuckled at its relevance.

We realised that some of our members must return soon to their previous assignments, but replacements arrived and our team grew. We began to ask God for openings on the other three islands.

Although the people insisted on celebrating important Islamic festivals with holidays, they gladly did the same for the Roman Catholic festivals too. One of these was the Day of Pentecost. Our mission leader, Norman Thomas, who had vigorously encouraged the ministry to the Comoro Islands from its outset, came to visit in a small mission plane. We asked the pilot to fly us to the second largest island, Anjouan. There we found the doctor in charge of the main hospital setting off for a picnic. 'Come with us,' he said with typical hospitality, 'and I'll answer all your questions.' We had a useful discussion which bore fruit in several openings a year later. One of the group had been drinking before the picnic. He started flirting with Joan and Sheila and I needed to continually get between him and the ladies! On a later visit to the island he saw us at the airport and said in astonishment, '*C'est incroyable!*' (It's unbelievable!), and again advanced towards Joan whom I felt shuddering behind me. He lived in a drunken haze. Later we heard he was working on a roof when he fell to his death. The sadness of 120,000 people on that island facing eternity without any knowledge of the Lord Jesus gnawed at our hearts.

God responded to our prayer to expand to the other islands in an unexpected way.

On a ward round I found a dead baby born in the night and dumped in a cot at the foot of a bed. No-one seemed to know about it. For the first time my anger exploded. I called Madame and demanded to know how the infant had died and why no-one had called me when the birth ran into difficulties. Shortly afterwards I attempted to turn an upside-down baby so that the head would present for delivery in a few days time. Madame complained to Sheila saying, 'You must not attempt to turn a baby in the womb. This is not done here. I

107

am in charge and if anything goes wrong, I am held responsible.' I discovered that, although government paid all hospital bills, many patients paid Madame as well to ensure adequate care!

After discussion with our team, I asked for a transfer and suggested Moheli. My request coincided with strong representations from the leaders on that small island. Their French doctor had left and they asked, 'Who will care for our fifteen thousand people? The *Mapinduzi* have only brought us loss!' The Minister, bowing to the political pressure, asked Sheila and later Justy Stoesz, a laboratory technician, to move there with Joan and me. Although we found a grubby hospital, rusting beds without bedding and few patients, we rejoiced in a warm welcome from the staff and in freedom to provide the care people needed.

Once more we began the process of cleaning. We scrubbed walls, bought mattresses and bedding, pestered the supply depot on Grande Comore for medicines, and persuaded the Vice-President (who came from Moheli) to authorise the purchase of surgical instruments. The little hospital filled.

We battled continually against rats which loved to chew the metal foil insulation of our stove. Rising one morning to make a cup of tea, I met two of them gazing at me through a perspex window in the oven door. As soon as I picked up a stick and opened the door they fled through the back of the stove and scampered out of the kitchen and into our bedroom where Joan sat reading. One ran up a four foot lampstand beside the bed, sat on the bulb, turned and smiled at me as if to say, 'If you smash this light, you know very well you'll not find another on Moheli.'

When flour was plentiful, the baker's servant trundled the bread along the dusty road to the hospital in a wheel barrow.

At times, imported foods like flour and sugar ran out, and we wondered what we would eat. But we soon realised that we could not starve. On operating days we opened our back door to find gifts of fish, rice and fruit, which patients' relatives had left either as tokens of gratitude or else as bribes to persuade us to do our best with the knife.

We tried to give more than medicine. An elderly teacher of the Koran required two operations. Before anaesthetising a patient I always enquired if he or she would like me to pray. No-one ever said 'no' and the *Mwalimu* (Teacher) was no exception. While he was recovering in the ward I visited him one afternoon and asked if he would like to hear a story from the *Injil*. I started with the two sons and watched his face light up. 'Tell me another,' he begged and I launched into The Good Samaritan. He enquired wistfully, 'Do you know any more?'

On the day before we arrived in Moheli a tragic accident occurred. A teenage soldier wrestled with another youth and two lads in uniform ran to his aid. One of them unslung his automatic rifle from his shoulder. A single shot in the air would scare the young fellow who dared to punch up a brave protector of the nation's newly-won freedom. His thumb fumbled with a switch on the weapon: turn it one way and the gun would discharge individual shots, switch it the other and a deadly stream would flow out. But which was which? He pressed the lever up. His index finger squeezed the trigger and froze in panic; he had never experienced automatic fire before. Sitting at her sewing machine inside her home Madame Amina's ears seemed to split. Immediately she thought of her children playing in the street and dashed out. A tremendous blow struck her legs, felling her to the ground. She noticed mud turning red around her shin and jagged white spicules sticking up from the shattered bone before she lost consciousness.

When she came round she found herself in a private ward of Moroni Hospital, her limb encased in plaster of paris and elevated on a pillow with five dark toenails peeping out of the embracing whiteness. Her surgeon, Dr Bill Barnett, came each day to peer at those toenails, talking quietly to his wife who translated into fluent French for the benefit of the plump Malagasy Sister and her Comorian nurses. This gentle, skilled, husband and wife team impressed her. The loving working relationship she saw at her bedside day by day stood out in stark contrast to most of the marriages she knew. It prepared the way for her friendship with Françoise.

Frances Mumford dropped in one day and explained to Amina that Mrs Barnett had asked her to visit as she and her husband were so busy they could rarely sit and talk to their patients. As their friendship developed, Amina became increasingly interested in her visitor's life. Frances explained that it revolved around the prophet known to Amina from the Koran as Issa. She explained that long ago she had trusted him to deliver her from sin, and he had given her peace and power. The Muslim from Moheli was fascinated.

After two months Amina returned home with her leg still in a heavy plaster and Frances asked Joan to visit. Often Joan would find visitors around the armchair in the courtyard where Amina sat with her heavy leg elevated. The disturbance of children, running, fighting and wanting to chat with Mum, would prevent serious talk. At other times they could read quietly from the French New Testament undisturbed. Joan asked one day, 'Do you know that the girl who works with my husband was married yesterday?' Amina nodded. 'It's the third time,' added Joan, 'and although she has borne four children she doesn't care for any of them herself.' The other lady replied, 'For many people here it's like a game: married today, divorced tomorrow. There's no assurance of a lasting love.'

'Assurance of a lasting love.' Joan had recently been gripped afresh by words in Romans chapter eight. She opened her New Testament and, after reading a few paragraphs, spoke of the assurance the believer can have of the Father's love that is certain and never changes. 'Perhaps I am not explaining very well,' she said once or twice. '*Je comprends, je comprends*,' replied Amina eagerly; 'please carry on.' Joan turned the page to read the final paragraph, 'I am persuaded that neither death, nor life, ... nor anything in all creation will be able to separate me from the love of God in Christ Jesus our Lord.' Amina was moved. '*C'est vrai, c'est vrai*' (It is true), she said several times. 'C'est merveilleux.'

*****

The new flag of the Republic of the Comores carried four stars, one for each island. In fact, the new nation consisted of three islands for the people of the fourth, Mayotte, chose to remain French. An abbreviated slogan, painted on a wall, summed up their attitude, 'Indep = Tyrran.' They mistrusted the people of Ngazidja (Grande Comore) and realised that, as a minority in the nation (their population of 30,000 was less than a tenth of the Comorian total), their share in trade, money and services would be minimal.

African news every day described King Hassan of Morocco's bold attempt to occupy Western Sahara by organising a massive, peaceful march to possess its mineral-rich deserts. Ali Soilihi determined on the same tactic for possessing Mayotte. Commandeering an aged aircraft of Air

Comores, he flew over to the island with his retinue and sent the plane back to Moroni for another load of demonstrators. They never arrived, for the French immediately covered the runway with petrol drums while Ali commenced his march. If he hoped for popular acclaim, he was disappointed, for the people derided him. Humiliated, he asked the authorities to kindly remove their drums so that his plane could land and take him home.

With small teams settled on Grande Comore and Moheli, I was eager to start in Mayotte. Miriam van Reenen enquired about returning to the Comoro Islands, bringing two other South African ladies with her. On the 16th June 1976 the BBC informed us of a huge riot of schoolchildren in Soweto, South Africa, during which six hundred lost their lives to police bullets. Unpopular already because of Apartheid, South Africa now became the international pariah. Even a South African entry stamp in a passport would disqualify you from entering any other African state, let alone a South African passport. When I broached the ladies' request to some Comorian friends they advised, 'Don't even ask the government of the Republic.' I talked to our team about sending them to Mayotte and some said, 'No; it's too risky. Firstly the Comorians will get upset if they hear we are helping the people of Mayotte who rejected their rule. And secondly they'll deplore the entry of South Africans.'

What should we do? The voice of reason said send them elsewhere. But had God called them, as they firmly believed? Had high tide arrived for Mayotte? Joan and I decided to fly across and meet the French *Resident* who governed the island. He assured us, 'We have no problem with South Africa, but we certainly do not need development workers. We simply send a list of our needs to France.' Unlike the Muslim government on the other islands, he had no objections to limited preaching. At least he promised temporary stay visas.

Miriam, Heather and Jeanette flew to Reunion and booked seats on the weekly military plane which hopped from there to Mayotte. Two days before departure date, the army decided to cancel all civilian bookings. The only other route lay through Moroni. Miriam sent a telegram to our team asking us to arrange for their stay over a weekend between flights. Frantically the team replied, 'Don't come!' but the message reached Reunion after they had left. When they arrived in Moroni, Immigration welcomed them and they spent two comfortable nights waiting for Air Comores to bring them to Mayotte.

Joan and I had already tramped the streets searching for suitable accommodation. We scoured the villages with the ladies and reluctantly settled for a filthy place which was far from suitable. The forlorn appearance depressed me: bare rooms with dirty walls, furnished by two beds and a chair we had purchased off the hotel scrap heap. A full pit latrine emitted a foul odour and a week's water supply in a forty-four gallon drum leaked like a sieve. Despite the importance of our next engagement, we wondered, 'Should we stay?' They calmly assured us they could manage. Nevertheless our hearts were heavy as we left them for our flight to Madagascar.

Aboard our Air Comores plane at Mayottes' little airport, one of the four engines refused to fire. The pilot told us to get out while he took off, climbed, accelerated in a dive until the fourth engine burst into life. Then he landed to pick us up without switching off. I wondered if this typified the shaky sort of start we had just made in our Mayotte ministry. Could it really take off and fly?

I need not have worried. Twenty years later the team continued to flourish in an island so prospering under French rule that the population had tripled. Believers were studying the New Testament and reading primers the ladies had prepared for them, as well as meeting together to worship and to witness.

*****

Telemaque Desamour, a Haitian laboratory technician, and his wife, Marie Ange, joined the team on Grande Comore with their young son, Telson, in April 1977, long after Joan and I had handed over the leadership. He and some others moved to the second largest island, Anjouan, to work in the main hospital there. Following several forced moves, the family was given a house where, for the third time, they cleaned the mess, dug out the septic tank, installed some simple furnishings and settled down. For seven months Telemaque worked in the hospital and quietly spoke to people about his friend, the great Messiah called Issa. Some showed interest, two or three believed.

On a Wednesday evening, while the family was decorating their Christmas tree, several soldiers hammered on the door and presented Telemaque with a letter commanding him to vacate the house and move to another. A young believer came on Boxing Day to assist with the move and the mountainous task of cleaning. The soldiers returned, more belligerent than before, and announced, 'You have broken the law by giving people Christian books. We have come to confiscate this literature and arrest you!' To his insistence that President Ali Soilihi had told our group that the state was secular, permitting us to tell Muslims about our religion and listen to what they said about theirs, they replied, 'That's all right for people of other religions but all Comorians are Muslims and must remain Muslims.' They took Telemaque away to their barracks where he was placed in his own room with a guard. Many of the soldiers came in twos and threes to talk about the reason for his arrest, giving him the chance to tell them freely about the Lord. After three days he was told to go home and prepare to visit Grande Comore with his family. A friendly soldier came secretly to tell him, 'Pack everything; they intend to expel you.'

On the main island, the family was split up. The soldiers allowed Norman Weiss, the Director of our group, to take Telson to his home while they took his parents to separate parts of a filthy jail, where they invited them to sleep on the bare cement floor. Telemaque shared his cell with fifteen others, some of whom showed the marks of beating. Around midnight they were released and allowed to return to their weeping little boy.

Two senior officials called the group to a meeting. One of them courteously said, 'You have worked with us in a harmonious way, but the Desamour incident is so serious that he must be repatriated.' Mr Weiss reminded them that the President had allowed us to share our faith and even invited us at one stage to broadcast on national radio. But it was to no avail; the Desamours must leave. Norman then said, 'In that case we have no option but for the whole group to depart.'

'We will be sorry,' they replied. 'We appreciate your work very much. Thank you.'

Our friend, the first known Christian in Grande Comore, had learnt much wisdom through bouts of persecution including imprisonment. Months after the team's departure he told us that the uninhibited witness of some had upset the government. In fact, someone spoke to the Director of the Kuwait Relief programme about the Lord Jesus in a way which he found offensive and he complained to the government. At the same time Muslim leaders objected to moves the President made against Muslims, which provoked them to complain that he allowed freedom to Christians while restricting them.

Perhaps we had been unwise in our zeal for the Lord. In expelling our seemingly defenceless team, the President may have fatally provoked that same Lord.

*****

In March 1978, two months after the expulsion, thirty-five French and Belgian mercenaries landed at night on a beach a few miles north of Moroni. Within hours they overran Grande Comore; within days Anjouan and Moheli fell and President Ali Soilih was shot, allegedly trying to escape. In early June I arranged to fly to Moroni, unsure of the reception awaiting us. Telegrams requesting landing permission went unanswered. As we overflew we watched soldiers run to man gun emplacements alongside the runway, and I felt the hairs on the back of my neck stand on end. We held our breath as the pilot taxied to the terminal, but no burst of gunfire greeted us. Instead the Chief of Immigration recognised me and welcomed us warmly.

Driving into the town centre we met overloaded pick-ups honking while their passengers sang in celebration of their freedom from the dictator. Ali Soilihi, in his effort to secular-ise the country and introduce Marxism, had forbidden the women to wear Muslim dress. Now, many were wrapped in black from head to foot – a symbol of religious liberty. The new leaders said this would be a new nation, no longer secular but Islamic, and I wondered if we would be allowed to return.

Bill and Laura Barnett flew over and settled into an old hotel. Eventually the government asked Bill to take over the hospital at the north end of the island, running it as a model for others to copy, and our work started up again.

A senior Muslim cleric consulted Bill about a leg infection which had resisted treatment for a year. Bill prayed, made a simple incision, applied ointment and the man recovered speedily. He later discovered that this man had engineered the expulsion of our team. As a result of that surgery he became a friend.

With a combination of great sensitivity to people and faithfulness to God, Bill said, 'Our service is our witness and, while we can't preach, we can pray and answer questions.' He normally only gave literature to people who asked and several did. An ex-patient returned from work one day and told his wife, 'I want you to make me some tea; something very important is about to happen to me.' She left him drinking and reading. Later she returned to find him dead in his chair with the New Testament open and spread across his face.

Slowly new team members arrived and spread across the islands.

*****

When we first went to Turkana the tide was out. God answered many prayers and it crept in. We thought that independence in Mozambique indicated a turn of tide, but it withdrew only to come flooding back seven years later. Our

Comorian experience was different: the circle of high and low tide revolved several times. Hopes for a country starved of the gospel rose when Miriam and Millie entered, but fell when revolution forced the Mission to withdraw them. Just five months later a team went back in, only to be driven out after two years. Following the mercenary invasion, a surgeon's scalpel, backed by prayer and compassion, once again prepared an entrance for the love of Christ. Using language still tinged with Koranic phrases, our Comorian Christian friend glimpsed God's strategy behind all this coming and going: 'If only the blind ones could see and feel the power and beauty of the Most High! They are like the thundering wave, splashing against the rocky shore. Slowly it moves away, for the blind one has taken no notice of its love, warmth and mercy. Yet it comes back, time and time again, for the Lord is Most Beneficent, the All-Powerful, Most Merciful.'

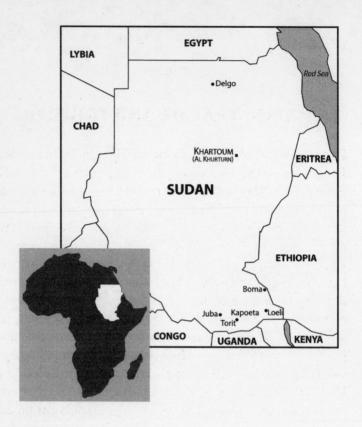

9

SUDAN: TRAUMA AND TRIUMPH

Pastor Nikolau placed me in the middle seat of his ancient Landrover, next to the young driver – a relative of his. He paused to say farewell to his wife, climbed in beside me and prayed that God would look after us. We pulled out from the dense shade of a mango tree and trundled past Torit town church on to the main road to South Sudan's capital, Juba. A whole year had passed since I responded to an invitation from Nikolau and his elder brother, Abednego, to join them in drawing up a development plan for their young group of churches. At that time they spent a fortnight showing me around their tiny denomination spread very thinly across three hundred miles of the south-eastern corner of the country where it borders on Ethiopia to the east and Kenya and Uganda to the south. At that time, and for nearly a year afterwards, the Comoro challenge demanded all our time.

When, in August 1976, the Comorian Vice-President implored Joan and me to remain on his island of Moheli, we felt compelled to say 'no'. Other team members had come to help his people and we felt we must move on to Sudan, where we had seen great needs. Now, after a month of extensive survey, I spent a quiet morning writing down some conclusions in preparation for meeting government leaders and other aid workers in Juba.

The track stretched out ahead of us, a yellow ribbon through thick bush with an occasional distant peak to break the monotony of the landscape. Lorries had pounded the shimmering sand into iron-hard corrugations, each a foot or more deep and about the same wide. A driver has two options: either he moves slowly so that the wheels negotiate each ridge and its matching ditch, or he speeds over their tops ignoring the intervening valleys. Ours chose the fast option – so fast that I felt unsafe and asked my host to slow down after the first few hundred yards. But manliness was at stake and, although the speedometer needle would drop for a few miles after every rebuke from the pastor, it soon spun steadily clockwise again. I gave up and settled back to the constant judder, broken by an occasional bang when we hit a larger than usual gap in the ridges.

After three hours we suddenly left the road, lurched into a gully, mounted a bank, narrowly missed a thick tree and ploughed for forty yards through grass taller than our vehicle. I knew we could not survive; a pit or a tree or a heap of rocks would surely break us to pieces. Thoughts raced through my mind, 'How will Joan and the youngsters cope ... and what about this promising work, just starting again after a lapse of years?' As trees flashed past, any one of which could have demolished our truck, I felt sad – not that I was unprepared for death – but because life on earth was so full of promise.

Amazingly the Landrover stopped and the right front wing subsided towards the ground. Seven of us climbed out, looked at each other and gasped. None had as much as a scratch or bruise! Next we walked round the front of the car and found a yawning gap where a wheel had sheered off. We searched along the road and discovered that it had careered on for another hundred yards until ending up among bushes. A young army lieutenant stopped and recognised Nikolau from a few years before when they had both been refugees in Uganda. With the help of his soldiers we lifted the wounded wing on to a jack to allow the driver to remove the buckled bumper and replace the wheel. With lights miraculously working, but no brakes, we limped slowly for ten miles to the bridge over the Nile, where guards forbade us to cross because the wartime curfew still prevailed, and we settled for the night on the ground beside our ailing Landrover. As I listened to the song of mosquitoes from the right side of a net, I thanked God for his deliverance and wondered if he too chuckled at my morbid thoughts earlier!

Other travellers did not get off so lightly. War had closed most garages so that drivers carried out amateur repairs as best they could, sometimes leaving vehicles unsafe. Rough roads took a heavy toll, often resulting in permanent injury or death. Victims of the fighting fared worst.

Nikolau introduced me to a church elder in a mountain village close to the Ugandan border. He had once been wealthy enough to own a lorry which supported his bakery. 'This is his truck,' said the pastor pointing to a burnt-out wreck parked at the side of the road; 'When the army swept through here they set it alight. Since then thieves have steadily hacked off pieces of tyre to fashion sandals.' The baker came out to greet us. A tattered shirt, patched trousers and bare feet spoke of poverty. But a wide smile, firm handshake and warm welcome witnessed to an inner wealth that no material loss could erase.

The baker typified God's church in South Sudan. Battered and often butchered, hard-pressed and persecuted, diminished but undaunted, the church had survived in places and, unknown to us at the time, was set to multiply in numbers and grow in maturity in three further decades of suffering.

*****

As we travelled, the brothers reminisced. Danger threatened Abednego in the mid-1960s when soldiers, representing the Muslim government, surrounded all the houses on one side of the main road through his home town, Kapoeta. They knocked at each door, called for the man of the house, and shot him as he appeared. Next day a friendly Egyptian warned Abednego, 'Tonight they'll slaughter all the men on your side. You sleep in my home.' A senior official told him he was unsafe even in that Muslim home and suggested he follow up his ambition of theological training outside the country. He was fortunate in obtaining a passport, and the godly Bishop Allison found money to fly his family to Kenya.

Others, including Nikolau, came on foot, encountering many dangers on the way. After graduating from Scott Theological College the brothers accepted school chaplaincies in Uganda until peace in 1972, when they returned to their devastated homeland.

Now, four years later, they dreamt of revived churches, schools, health care, a farm to support pastors and a Bible school to train them. They led me round their huge parish and, as we travelled, we asked God to show us his vision and how to clothe it with projects and plans.

In January 1977 Joan joined me. The country, greened by recent rain, welcomed us. Its red track cut through miles of long grass and low acacias while, never far off, mountains stabbed the skyline. Hammerkops, storks and a heron flapped lazily away as we approached them. We praised our God for such beauty and resumed our practice of prayer as we trundled on, 'Lord, please guide us in the work.' We discussed all the possibilities with him. Our children away in their boarding schools often came to mind: 'Lord, Bless Mary, Helen and Donald, separated so far from us for the sake of your

Kingdom.' We poured out all the details of our concerns and felt the peace he promised.

We found that one of the main tribes, the Taposa, spoke a language almost identical to Turkana. Quickly Joan adjusted to some of the differences so that, whenever a few people gathered, she would strike up a chorus. People turned to listen, registered surprise as they recognised the words, beamed broadly and joined in. Best of all, after one of the pastors had talked simply about the Lord, they walked away happily singing the song they had just learnt. Joan longed that they read the Word of God themselves and prepared a primer which one of the aid agencies promised to print. But before they could get round to it, war broke out again and Joan's book suffered the fate of so much well-intentioned development in Sudan.

We came to a poor, tumbledown village and set up a simple clinic. Half the population scratched at scabies and many rubbed the pus out of infected eyes. One fifth of my 241 patients suffered from diarrhoea. Malnutrition and malaria complicated most diagnoses and probably accounted for the 80% of children who presented enlarged livers and spleens. I wondered if shortage of food contributed also to the mass of arthritic joints. Most disease in this and other villages seemed preventable with attention to nutrition and hygiene. Only a very fast pair of legs could have prevented one disorder in my list, 'Pain at the site of an old ostrich bite!'

We wandered around the village. Women, dressed only in skirts, and men (clad in much less) greeted us. In the midst of poverty we saw grain spread out in preparation for beer making, and old ladies smoking bamboo-stemmed pipes. We met a male nurse with a background of three months training. He showed us his little clinic, with mud walls and grass roof like the rest of the buildings in the community. I enquired, 'Where are the medicines?' He waved an expressive hand towards the bare shelves and said, 'This is all I have.'

The cause of the gospel had not fared much better than health care. Before the government expelled all missionaries by the early sixties, some workers had begun to make an impression. As we travelled we kept coming across evidence of church life in the past: a vibrant believer like our baker friend; others, less lively, but still glad to bear a new name given in baptism; a church building blasted by rockets; missionary residences reduced to concrete foundations; a once-precious water tank riddled with bullet holes. Abednego and Nikolau told us of faithful men and women who had lived out the life of Christ in these remote villages and taught about his love. Surely seed lay here, awaiting another team of harvesters.

Driving for thousands of miles around Sudan I began to feel that nerves extended beyond the confines of my body and out to the suffering parts of the vehicle. A sharp crack of a broken spring, the hiss of air from a punctured tyre, steam rising in a cloud from a radiator clogged with grass, the thud of a rock striking the gearbox in the belly of the car – all seemed to jar somewhere around my solar plexus. Often they presaged many hours of hard labour in the blazing sun, with Joan loyally encouraging me to keep on.

We drew some (rather unkind) comfort from others who fared worse. Water washed around our feet as we ploughed boldly through a swamp for several hundred yards. When we emerged we found two Austrians sitting in chairs beside their dripping Combi, waiting for it to dry out. The flood had doused their engine and left them locked in mire until a kind Samaritan pulled them out. Further on we read a notice beside

a temporary bridge, 'For Landrovers and light vehicles only.'
The driver of a Mercedes lorry had ignored the warning and
we saw his vehicle beneath the bridge, its wheels forlornly
reaching into the air and the river washing through the
upturned cab. As darkness fell we met another lorry and
wondered how long it would survive. Overloaded with
soldiers it listed heavily to one side. They asked us to drive
behind them so they could benefit from our headlights, for
they had none of their own.

The army and police appeared everywhere. In any little
town we had to stop and show travel documents. 'You must
sign the Alien Register,' they always commanded. One
constable brought a huge book labelled 'Lost Property' and
told us to fill in details of our vehicle and our destination.
When I asked where we should write our names, he looked
puzzled and then said, 'There's no column in the book for
that so you had better leave it out.' Patiently our Sudanese
friends always chatted for a while until the man in uniform
decided to move a pole blocking the road and wave us
through.

*****

In Kapoeta we met the Colonel commanding a large district.
His wife had accompanied him from their home many
hundreds of miles away to this seemingly remote place and
foreign culture, where she knew no-one. The strain finally
broke her on Christmas Eve and she shot herself. After forty
days of mourning the widower planned a memorial meal and
generously invited us. Pastor Abednego said, 'Let's go; we
may be able to help them with the Word of God.' So we sat
down on his verandah with twenty army officers and local

traders. The Sudanese ladies came in to greet us, humbly shuffling on their knees, before waiting on us. Joan, embarrassed at being the only woman at the table, still enjoyed the meal. Our safari diet had consisted largely of bread, tasting stale and acrid from the weevils which lived in all the flour, augmented occasionally by gazelle meat shot by Abednego. Here the Colonel served up Kissera – a delicious millet dough enfolding a tasty chicken and tomato stew. Despite the good fare, gloom struck us all and the pastor never felt free to speak about Jesus.

A couple of days later the pastor and I left for a journey to the Kenyan border. As we planned some hard driving through thick bush, Joan decided to stay in our temporary home in the town and to work on her primer. Early in the afternoon shots interrupted her thoughts. Outside she could see people running in excitement and terror. A Sudanese friend heard the news on the radio. He told her, 'People in Juba have risen against the government. It could spread here. Sit down, Mama, and keep calm.' That night the thump of drums kept her awake. Feeling utterly at sea and terribly alone, she focused her mind: 'The Lord is my shepherd, I shall lack nothing .... Even though I walk through the valley of the shadow of death, I will fear no evil, for you are with me.' 'He who dwells in the shelter of the Most High will rest in the shadow of the Almighty. I will say of the Lord, "He is my refuge and my fortress, my God, in whom I trust."' She thought on verse after verse, on and on through the hours of darkness, until the pounding in her ears dimmed and an uneasy sleep stilled her thoughts.

The news took two days to reach us in our remote wilderness. Fearfully we returned to Kapoeta, only to find that the rebellion did not spread out of Juba. Air Force officers had planned a coup to take place simultaneously a few days later in Khartoum and Juba, but timing failed because enthusiasts jumped the gun in the southern capital and troops loyal to the government quashed it.

Later we heard of an AIM pilot who was visiting Juba at the time of the attempted coup. Anxious to save his plane, he took advantage of a lull in the fighting to make a dash for the airport. An armed soldier stopped him and ordered him to return to town. Anxiety and lack of familiarity with the gears in a borrowed van may have combined to cause tragedy, for when Hal thrust the gear lever into position, the vehicle lurched forward instead of backwards and the soldier shot him. The bullet punctured a neck artery and Hal died soon after reaching Juba hospital.

In Kapoeta the Colonel courteously advised us to avoid any travel for a week. Then we decided to head off in the opposite direction from Juba. We stepped back forty years in time to another war when European nations fought over the remote wastes between Kapoeta and Sudan's mountainous border with Ethiopia. For half the year the road to Loeli forms part of a vast swamp. In order to maintain the border against the Italian army on the other side, the British cut a road through many miles of thorn bushes and paved it with uneven stones. The thorns had grown across the track again, the branches arching to meet in the middle where they embraced the Landrover, screeching as we forced our way underneath. Decades of storms had dislodged stones – many the size of cannonballs – and juggled them into an uneven carpet, over which we crept in second gear, jerking as each wheel struck a new rock. The incessant jolting and shrill scratching reduced Joan to tears. We stopped under a tree to check our springs and the sight of several fractures made me feel like weeping too.

But we achieved our goal – a meeting with a tribe at Loeli who called themselves *Nyangatom* (meaning Yellow Elephants). We settled in a decaying police post, deserted many years before, on the shoulder of a hill enfolding a freshwater spring. Nyangatom axes had been hacking at roof timbers – which made valuable firewood – with the result that most buildings opened to the sky and, from those whose roofs survived, corrugated iron sheets flapped in the breeze awaiting the next storm to sweep them away into the plains. For half the year the police had looked out across a swamp, impassable except to people who know where to walk. The Nyangatom, of course, love their wilderness and laughingly told us of a constable; 'He found the situation so dreary that he hiked through the marshes for eighty-two miles to Kapoeta, flung his rifle down and deserted.'

Although their language sounded even closer to Turkana than Taposa, they insisted that the Turkana fought against them as bitter enemies. Many of the men carried old rifles. I asked a young fellow called Philip how he obtained his weapon. He replied, 'I walked eleven cattle to Addis Ababa where I exchanged them for a rifle and ten rounds.' After hearing the pastor preach he proudly informed us, 'I am a Christian. I have changed my name.' Realising he referred to baptism when converts often choose a Bible name, I enquired, 'What is the meaning of these columns of short scars down the front of your chest and tummy?' He boasted, 'Each line signifies a Turkana I killed.' We imagined the horror in a Turkana home: a sudden cry at dawn, 'enemies'; then flashing spears and blazing guns force the outnumbered defenders to flee, leaving the weak. When the slaughter of women and children is over, the warriors round up the Turkana cattle and goats and race home to carve columns of medals on their chests. We wondered if Philip knew anything of Jesus' command to love our enemies.

Two of Joan's dresses disappeared while we were attending to sick people. We immediately stopped our work. I said, 'We come all this way to help you with medicine and you steal our clothes!' Innocence spread across every face. Trying not to laugh I announced, 'No more treatment until they come back.' After lunch they returned as surreptitiously as they had departed.

We got them singing Turkana choruses and told them the wonderful message of Jesus, searching for the lost and dying on our behalf. Bowed heads responded, '*Iteni, iteni*' (true). But we questioned if one hearing could change their lives. To make our next visit easier we cleared an airstrip. Yet when I touched down in a light Cessna Aircraft a few months later all the people had moved away and we asked ourselves, 'When will they ever hear again?'

We treated our Landrover wounds before skirting the foot of a great mountain range for another gruelling 125 miles of disused tracks northwards. Wild game delighted Abednego who used his rifle to obtain meat for our table. We paused to admire a family of vultures; mother balanced anxiously on the edge of her treetop nest while, beneath her, several open beaks waited hungrily for father to return with food.

A herd of several hundred buffalo tempted me to pursue them until, when I had foolishly driven to within forty yards, they all stopped, turned and glared at us. I reversed smartly and fled.

Clawing our way up a zigzag track in low gear, we reached an old fortified army post called Boma, now occupied by a section of Sudanese police. Then we passed gun emplacements with thick walls of loose stones built by the

British to protect their weapons against Italian invaders. When the enemies arrived from Ethiopia, they were so exhausted that they gladly surrendered and enjoyed British hospitality. We found ourselves on a fertile plateau among peaks. Boma itself is the ancient core of a volcano, spiking upwards hundreds of feet. Two constables kindly climbed on to the Landrover to guide us through long grass to a grove of mango trees sheltering a tumbledown rest house erected long ago by a District Commissioner. Here we met linguists, Jon and Barbara, from the Wycliffe Bible Translators, with their baby – wearied by two days creeping across the plains. Two men from ACROSS (The African Committee for the Rehabilitation of South Sudan) were investigating the needs of the local Murle people. In our wanderings in Sudan we always received a warm welcome from such groups. They invariably met us as allies rather than competitors – offering hospitality, giving information and advice, helping with fuel and spare parts, even lending a Landrover on one occasion.

The Africa Inland Church had never worked among the Murle. Five other tribes live in this border area, none of whom knew anything of the Lord Jesus, and we wanted to contact them. But the police forbade us to go further. They explained, 'We sent a Murle constable to count potential voters from the neighbouring Kichepo tribe. Sadly he drank too much and commanded the Kichepo to surrender their guns. They promptly shot him. Inter-tribal war broke out and has claimed twenty-one lives to date, forcing the Murle to move their homes alongside our post.'

Over many weeks of travel we attempted to follow every track known to the pastors or marked on old maps. We encountered seventeen ethnic groups, of whom twelve, like the Nyangatom and the five tribes along the border, possessed no church whatsoever. In the remaining five, small flocks of believers fought against great odds with the help of very few shepherds. Everywhere poverty and destruction wrung our hearts.

We always returned eventually to Torit where the pastors welcomed us to their house beside the airstrip. Often at dawn I rose to wander along its length, asking God to show his plan for our work in this part of Sudan, laying before him all the possibilities we had discussed, first with the church leaders and then with government ministers and department heads in Juba. The pastors shared our primary concern for leadership development and asked us to open a Bible School as soon as possible. We all grieved over the desperate poverty everywhere and longed to alleviate suffering. But, in the long term, we knew that mature believers are God's best gifts to any society. They will imitate his pity and draw on his power to tackle distress in all its forms.

During the days before the ejection of missionaries in the sixties, the Mission ran a rudimentary hospital and several small clinics for treatment of disease, and the pastors thought we should re-establish these. They recognised, however, that such a programme would be too costly for a church as poor as their own and asked us to consult with government and tie our health care programme into theirs. In Juba the Director of Primary Health Care responded warmly to our interest. He showed us his plan for developing complexes of four or five small units, each under the charge of a local villager, whom the community chose and the government trained to immunise, teach simple hygiene and treat the dozen or so commonest diseases which accounted for about 80% of sickness. A more highly trained nurse would run a dispensary in each complex, supervise the village workers and try to ensure that supplies got through. 'Maybe your nurses could help in that way,' he suggested. In the uncertain conditions of Sudan, we immediately recognised the wisdom of channelling our skills through local villagers so that, whenever we had to leave, something useful would remain. He produced a map and marked out two complexes for us near Kapoeta and Torit. We asked if we could later consider a third at Loeli and he readily agreed.

The pastors deplored the lack of schools and asked for our assistance. Again we felt that our greatest contribution would lie in assisting Sudanese teachers to become effective in sharing their knowledge. Another helpful agency in the area, the Norwegian Church Relief, had already built schools and planned others. While we shared the concern of the pastors to develop agriculture, we questioned their concept of a farm for the financial support of church workers. We preferred to look for agriculturalists, humble enough to sit for months with the villagers learning the language and the skills they already possessed. Then, when they had earned the respect of the community, they could suggest ways of improving the gardens. Better crops would improve nutrition in the community as well as giving income for Christians to support their ministers.

I kept saying to myself, 'Our time may be short, so keep priorities clearly in mind. Bring people to Christ, plant churches and encourage leaders, so that the people of God will continue to serve their communities in all the ways their Master might choose. Seek missionary communicators who will learn language, understand culture, make friends and gain acceptance – patient enough for a long stay and yet flexible enough to move at a moment's notice. They will measure success not by the numbers of buildings erected or even of people trained, but by the vitality of the church ten years after all missionaries have departed.'

As I asked God to send people of this calibre, a refugee pastor demonstrated the sort of sacrificial humility Sudan demands of guests. An AIM teacher, seconded to ACROSS in Juba, invited me to a refugee church a few miles south of the city. Although the people dressed poorly, many without shoes, and worshipped in a shack which consisted of a frame of sticks supporting a grass roof, they welcomed us with warm Christian hospitality. After the service I sat talking to the pastor, Alfonse. He told me, 'We came from Zaire (now the Democratic Republic of Congo). When mercenaries crushed a revolt there, rebels came to my church, pointed guns at me and demanded, "You must come with us to teach us the words of God." They led me to Central African Republic but the people there would not let us stay. Slowly we walked 600 miles east to the slums of Juba. Our reputation had gone ahead and, when we tried to settle, we attracted the blame for every crime committed in the city.'

Alfonse could have returned home but he had grown to love his flock. He brought them out of Juba until they came to empty land where they could build homes and plant gardens. He wanted us to meet the evangelists he was training. As I shook their hands and looked into their smiling faces, I realised these murderers now walked with God – forgiven, accepted and transformed. I marvelled at the power of our Lord to work in the midst of chaos and crime.

*****

The first to volunteer were veterans, Ray and Betty. Driving in with supplies in two vehicles, Ray's heavy lorry dislodged a landmine which Betty's small truck then detonated.

Mercifully, although the explosion tossed them into the air, neither she nor the truck sustained injury. They lived for eighteen months in tents at the foot of fertile mountains close to Uganda and began to build a Bible School. When Joan and I visited them, Ray showed us foundations of buildings and his brick kiln, then his garden which was already supplying their table. He was preaching in the Bangala language he had learnt as a child of missionary parents in Zaire, and in the simplified form of Arabic used in South Sudan. Rain poured down on us and I could understand why one of their favourite audio-tapes consisted entirely of laughter, with no words at all. Eventually the Pontiers rejoiced to see Pastor Nikolau installed as Principal.

Bill Anderson, who had once served with us in Turkana, led our new team. Nurse Martha and teacher Barbara returned to their original homes, rebuilt after almost total destruction. Ross and Ruth, also ex-Turkana, joined the pioneer group. The team grew to number thirty-four and some of our initial goals seemed in sight. Through many agencies, across South Sudan bulldozers scraped new roads, drilling rigs bored deep wells, educators developed a variety of skills and fields produced food. Levels of health and nutrition rose while the horrors of war receded.

But in 1983 the window of peace began to close. The Islamic government in Khartoum adopted an increasingly militant attitude towards the south. In addition to the old north/south confrontation with its largely religious motivation, ancient tribal animosities revived and southerner fought southerner. The rule of law failed, and gangs of bandits turned their guns on anyone they thought might possess something worth taking. Missionaries withdrew early in 1985, only to return a few months later. But as fighting escalated they abandoned the remoter centres and concentrated in the towns. Eventually only Juba remained safe.

In Nairobi I received a request to meet a small plane carrying Lanny and Janis, our new team leader in Sudan and his wife. Lanny was devastated. His first words seared my heart, 'It's too much Dick.' Choking with grief he told me parts of his story which he later clarified, 'Driving south of Kapoeta this morning we crossed a steep dry river bed. As I shifted gear to climb the bank, I heard a shot from my side of the Landrover and felt the tyre blow out. I turned to Janis and said, "That was a shot and...." Before I could finish the sentence I heard a second shot and saw a look of pain cross her face as the bullet passed through the vehicle and into her back. She fell forward against the dashboard and I saw the gaping flesh wound. I accelerated up the ridge and raced on for another few kilometres until I could no longer control the steering wheel due to the damaged tyre. I stopped. We bandaged the wound and then changed the tyre. With the help of a Sudanese Christian Janis was able to sit up as we drove on, but the pain was agonising for the road was rough.'

Lanny drove on for an hour and a half to the nearest health centre run by Norwegian Church Aid where there was a radio and an airstrip. A doctor arrived two hours later in response to his call. He finished his story, 'We were flown to Juba and thence to Kenya. Janis lost consciousness in Juba and died about half way to Nairobi.'

As we wept, I wrestled with an agonising sense of responsibility, for I had first asked them to work in Sudan. But God seemed to say, 'They came at my command, not yours.'

Lanny eventually returned to Sudan. Years later he talked about his experience in a meeting and a man in the audience told him that he was due to fly to Nairobi on that fateful day but gave up his place to make room for Lanny and Janis. Having seen their distress, he was touched that Lanny came back to serve Sudan. Another hearer recalled the Muslim Customs Officer who said, 'Now we know you love Sudan to return after such a tragic experience.'

*****

Finally the government expelled our remaining workers. They flew out of Juba, spiralling up from the airport to escape surface-to-air missiles of a rebel army surrounding the city.

Chaos again reigned. Fire consumed clinics and houses which our team had patiently erected over several years. War and drought claimed thousands of lives. Millions more abandoned their homes and gardens, moving to settle around the cities of Sudan, north and south, in abject poverty made worse by government harassment. Others crossed boundaries to erect huts in refugee camps where at least they could receive aid from international agencies. Wherever they settled, Christians spread the Word of God and multitudes believed, forming new congregations, opening schools and begging us to help train pastors and teachers.

Over the last three troubled decades of the Millenium, the number of AIC Sudan congregations rose from thirty to over a hundred. Their Sudanese missionaries, augmented by several couples from Kenya and Congo, crossed cultural barriers to plant new churches among people who knew nothing of the Lord. From the deserts around Khartoum, a thousand miles south to Juba, east to the remote mountain fastness of Boma and across international boundaries in massive camps, precious saints – often unshod and clad only in rags – lifted hands to God in joyful worship.

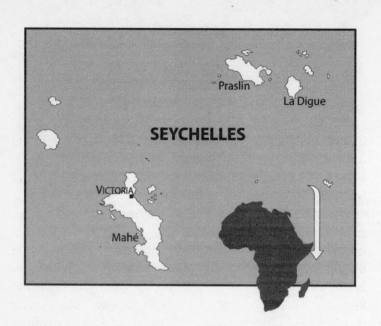

10

SEYCHELLES: POTS AND PLANS

Statistics in Seychelles baffled me. A senior government official claimed, '99% of our people are Christians' and yet a top church leader complained, '75% of our babies are bastards.'

The museum in Victoria, the capital of this tiny nation, gave me a clue. A picture portrayed the arrival of the first missionaries. A friar with tonsured head and brown flowing habit had just stepped on to the beach from a ship which still lay at anchor behind him. Already he was busy baptising kneeling islanders. He appeared to commit the classic missionary mistake of proselytising without first persuading: of presuming that outward allegiance indicated inward change.

The Far East Broadcasting Association (FEBA) reached this newly-independent nation in 1971 to serve a vast population who lived in a wide arc bordering the Indian Ocean from South Africa through the Middle East as far as India. The radio workers found themselves living among people who called themselves Christian, but appeared unaware of Christ's saving power in their lives. As commitment to their specialist ministry demanded most of their time, they asked AIM to consider joining them to focus on the spiritual needs of the Seychellois.

Norman Thomas, the International General Secretary of AIM, requested Paul and Betty Stough, with long experience in Zaire and Kenya, to investigate this challenge. On their return from the islands they recommended that AIM work with the well-established Anglican church. Norman then suggested that Joan and I develop a programme.

In November 1976 a Super VC 10 belonging to British Airways whisked us across a thousand miles of ocean to land between palm trees and brilliant blue sea on the new airport of Mahe Island. We found our way to a cheap waterfront hotel where hot humidity hit us like a hammer. The tide withdrew to leave a deposit of garbage on the muddy foreshore. Joan's head throbbed; my skin ran with sweat while Shirley Bassey sang from a nearby radio, 'This is a lovely way to spend an evening.'

Next morning we tried to phone FEBA but failed, so we decided to walk until a brisk downpour forced us into a taxi. Our road twisted upwards through forested hillsides, beside granite outcrops, past a secluded home to which the Cypriot Archbishop Makarios had once been exiled by the British government, and into the modern radio station. The rain cleared revealing fabulous glimpses of the ocean six hundred feet below. FEBA's director, John Wheatly, was recovering from flu and trying to prepare for a flight to the UK that evening. Even so he sat down to explain the religious scene and to suggest people we should meet.

High on John's list was Bishop Briggs. We met him outside the little church in the town centre – a small elderly man whom I first thought to be a retired planter. He cordially invited us into his office and called his Archdeacon to join us. They belonged to the High Church tradition of Anglicanism and feared that another viewpoint would cause confusion. Perhaps to test us they broached the subject of prayers for the dead. The Archdeacon asked, 'Don't you think we should express our fellowship with the departed?' and the Bishop expressed surprise at our view that death ends all opportunity for a sinner to turn to the Saviour. He gently implied presumption on our part, 'If you died today would you be ready? Are you perfect enough now to enter heaven?' A clinching argument in a population where nine out of ten people are Roman Catholic was, 'Christians ask us to pray for their dear deceased. If we refuse, they will turn to the Catholics.' Even though we differed on important issues, Joan and I felt drawn to these two sincere men. As we parted, the Bishop wistfully admitted, 'Your approach with an emphasis on personal belief is something we need here.'

When you seek to enter a new population with the precious gospel, you have to explore every avenue. In Seychelles we kept running into a blank wall because, as one senior government official said, 'We are a Christian country; why should we accept more missionaries?' We wondered if the schools might welcome our teachers, but no, they had enough. What about health care personnel, water engineers, agriculturalists? People smiled and shook their heads. For a while we received encouragement along the line of opening a bookshop but then ran into strange obstructions – inexplicable until a friend in Immigration told us that the President himself (ousted soon afterwards in a coup) owned the main bookshop; 'Do you think he will welcome competition?'

We wandered all round Victoria, the only real town in this island nation of 60,000 people. French blood mingled with African slave genes, augmented by Indian, Malagache and Chinese, to produce a fascinating variety. We looked into a dark brown face to meet clear blue eyes. A man appeared European in every way except for his tightly curled African hair – which was blonde!

We watched scantily-clad tourists, who provide the

Seychelles with their main source of foreign capital, thronging the shops and market, packing the buses and taxis, and ambling along streets lined with colonial-style, corrugated-iron buildings. We walked to the end of a new pier in glorious sunshine and looked back towards the town. Yachts bobbed at anchor in blue sea; smart new buildings carpeted reclaimed land along the shore; the old town clustered around the tiny Anglican and huge Roman Catholic cathedrals and then trickled up valleys leading into forested hills; and towering over all was the massive granite face called Les Trois Freres.

We took a boat across to two other islands and warily watched a menacing shark's fin which followed us for a while. A lackadaisical holiday spirit occasionally crept up on us, only to be displaced by the disturbing conviction that the tide was changing for this beautiful land and the destiny of many people depended on finding the right channel for the gospel. Wherever we wandered we cried, 'Lord show us your will for our ministry here.'

Senior government officers received us courteously. The Permanent Secretary to the Ministry of Education and Social Services viewed our offer of help with circumspection. Then he shared a problem, 'We have a thousand fifteen-year-olds who drop out of school every year and cannot find work. Could you not establish craft training – perhaps pottery?' His request took us by surprise but as we prayed about it we realised that this was the only positive lead we had. I went back to him a few days later and promised to share his suggestion with our leaders.

Norman Thomas reacted with his usual enthusiasm. Hitherto he and I had found our leaders fully supportive of the new outreach emphasis. But some hesitated now. In an executive committee they asked, 'Since 1975 we have

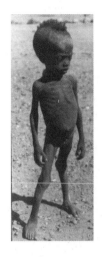

← Famine

The Poor →

← Man Suffering
from Eye Infection

Typical Turkana People →

Singing a Turkana Song with Gospel
Recordings

Turkana Clinic

Anderson Family
Picture, Kenya 1983 →

Reading the first
gospel in Turkana

↓

Safari Camp:
Ewei Preaching

↓

initiated new thrusts into the Comoro Islands, Mozambique and Sudan. Should we not pause to consolidate? Perhaps our existing work will suffer if we pour resources into more new countries.' Two mission elders even warned about the dangers of empire building! Prudent concern for established ministry vied with a pressing passion for the unreached.

I felt a pain deep inside me. Confronted by thousands who needed the message of Jesus, I empathised with Jeremiah when common sense cautioned silence, 'His word is in my heart a burning fire, shut up in my bones. I am weary of holding it in; indeed I cannot' (Jer. 20:9).

As we asked God to guide us we realised that the two concerns need not conflict: we must simply discern his will in each situation and obey. The leaders agreed that we move ahead. One statistic that later proved them right relates to the number of our serving missionaries. Early in 1976 the active missionary membership of AIM stood at 603. In the following ten years we entered eight new countries and the number swelled to 790. Less than half the additions worked in these eight countries. So the Lord honoured our leaders' faith by increasing resources for both the established and the new ministries, confirming the conviction that revived vision for the lost will always revitalise vigour all round.

*****

The Permanent Secretary wanted assurances before submitting our proposals to the Government, 'What personnel have you available and how much money do you plan to invest?' I knew of no potters in AIM and we certainly possessed no spare cash. He was not too impressed when I explained the great statement of Hudson Taylor that 'God's work done in God's way will never lack God's supply.'

145

Launching a new project for a mission such as ours often results in a puzzle. Before you can get the consent of the authority concerned, such as government or church, its leader wants to know that people and money are ready. If you encourage personnel to volunteer they ask, 'Have you got the go-ahead from the authorities? And what financial provision have you made?' Potential donors likewise ask if you have permission and personnel before they consider committing their money. Despite the Permanent Secretary's scepticism the answer lies in our relationship with God. If we live close enough to him, we can expect him to reveal his plans. Of course we make mistakes, but careful thought and prayer often result in the confidence we need to answer each enquirer, 'Yes, we're sure we can obtain all we need.' To our joy the official accepted our assurance.

I asked our Mission Director in Kenya about personnel and he mentioned a teacher who was a potter and keen to use his ceramic skills in missionary service. We approached Jack and Bunny and they agreed to go. The Lord was already nudging two veterans in Zaire, Stanley and Carmel, towards Seychelles. They felt God calling them to give a final two years of service in administration and Bible teaching. Some generous donors looked sympathetically at our plans and promised help.

We drew up a project for establishing a ceramics training centre for school-leavers, for which the Mission would provide personnel and capital but the Government would budget for maintenance, utilities and wages for Seychellois employees. We planned to train local staff to take the programme over in eight years.

On the seafront we found an old club building which had once been a fish market. The club, which was government owned, had fizzled out and no-one was using the facilities. A FEBA engineer looked it over and pronounced the building sound. So we asked the government for it and they said yes. Reading my diary now leaves me breathless. We chased around the island searching for accommodation, visited estate agents, discussed building plans for the centre in a multitude of government offices, negotiated details of an agreement with the government – and all in the context of immense kindness from Christian friends, especially in FEBA.

Our next visit lasted long enough to see how abundantly God had answered our prayers. We hardly recognised the tumbledown club in its restored beauty. Jack demonstrated the use of potters' wheels and showed off the kiln, initiating us into the art of preparing pots from the beginning. We watched students mix the primitive clay by trampling it underfoot in a large trough, plonk a soft ball on to the potter's wheel, gently mould the spinning mass into some shape, stack the new vessel into a kiln for firing, paint on glaze, apply intense heat again and finally place it in the shop window facing on to the main thoroughfare out of Victoria where hopefully it would tempt some tourist to buy an authentic piece of Seychellois art.

In the evening we joined the weekly Bible study in the home of Stanley and Carmel Kline. Stanley introduced us to a plumber, two policemen, a maintenance man from Cable and Wireless, a newspaper employee, a laboratory technician, a radio engineer and his girl friend, a Burmese couple working for IMF, their daughter on vacation from London University and their engineer son on holiday from Burma. Mostly they were new Christians, hungry for God's Word. We sensed the skilled touch of the divine potter.

*****

Stanley noticed a closed Anglican church not far from his home and offered his services to Bishop Briggs, explaining that though a Presbyterian, he was ordained and had often conducted services in Zaire. 'Yes, it's true we lack sufficient ministers to lead services there,' the Bishop responded; 'But you're not an Anglican. How could you lead the communion?'

Stanley replied, 'You can send along an Anglican to conduct the occasional communion and leave me with the simple service of morning prayer.' And so quiet diplomacy opened another opportunity. Eventually, long after Stanley had completed his two years in the country, the trust he had helped build resulted in a new Seychellois Bishop appointing an AIM missionary to run the training programme for new ministers.

When the converts in a fellowship meeting decided to establish a church, they put us in an awkward spot for we had undertaken that we would not start a new denomination, and one of our American potters taught the group so often as to appear an obvious leader. The Bishop criticised us for reneging on our promise. On my next visit our team discussed the matter and concluded that, although we would not plant a new group of our own, we would be available to serve any Seychellois congregation which asked for our help as long as we could teach the Bible in all its transforming truth.

At the end of eight years we fulfilled our commitment to provide trained local potters to lead the centre. But the Government wished to incorporate it into a new Polytechnic and we took our hands off – as we had agreed at the start. Instead our little team set up a potters' cooperative society on new premises and continued to nurture men and women until they could run the business themselves.

Over the course of fifteen years from the time we started,

hundreds of Seychellois came into a living relationship with Christ. None of our team would claim responsibility for this movement of God's Spirit, but probably all played a part by prayer and teaching. They also injected skills which enabled some to make a living. And who can measure the good effect of introducing a new art form into a culture emerging into post-colonial dignity?

I do not know how many Seychellois babies are now born out of wedlock but I am sure of this: many sinners have found the Saviour and many families have entered his kingdom.

11

LEADERSHIP: WITH JESUS IN THE STORMS

In Turkana, Peter Mualuko once explained the difficulties of leadership: 'A bull leads his column of cattle up a narrow, winding track to a summit. There he pauses to ponder the path in front of him. He asks himself, "what is the safest way down the other side, ... where might leopards or lions hide, ... can we find water and grazing?" Unaware of the new situation which the bull sees, the cattle behind simply expect to plod on as before and express their irritation at the delay by butting his hind quarters with their sharp horns.' The Pastor paused and then concluded, 'A leader must expect perplexity ahead and pain behind.'

As Associate Secretary for Outreach I had been mainly concerned with the way ahead. Although each situation presented its own unique set of problems, Joan and I developed a system which served us well: consider a new area or group of unreached people, discover all you can, consult others who are concerned, explore opportunities – if possible on the ground and for as long as it takes – draw up a strategy, present it to International Council for discussion and approval, seek and launch a new team and establish a team leader. The most urgent challenge which faced us and the developing teams was fervent prayer for every step.

Leadership meant stepping out ahead of others, discerning God's plans, motivating team members and fostering their determination to stick with the task when all the circumstances shouted, 'Give up!' We could study the perplexing path ahead without the pressures from followers behind, for at first we were on our own and, when we succeeded in establishing a new team, we delegated its direction to a team leader while we explored a fresh challenge.

Now change loomed again – and we hesitated. In 1978 the International Council asked me to take over from Norman Thomas as International General Secretary (IGS). I had worked closely with Norman and had come to admire him, particularly for the patient manner in which he handled those horns butting from behind.

Norman had held the job for six years. Before his appointment four autonomous councils, based in Australia, Canada, UK and USA, sent missionaries to serve under five other autonomous councils in Central African Republic, Kenya, Tanzania, Uganda and Zaire. In 1972 delegates from each of these leadership bodies decided that the Mission needed one 'final authoritative body ... to provide close and effective co-operation and spiritual unity between its councils'. This International Council (IC) would formulate and co-ordinate general policy and practice of the Mission and would 'exercise jurisdiction over the Mission's work through the IGS'. They appointed Norman to this position.

This move seemed sensible, for we needed to relate as a unified body to the mass of new churches growing in our traditional areas of ministry and to multitudes of peoples still outside the range of the gospel. Also the increased ease of travel and communication made it attainable. In practice, however, many members of the Mission felt comfortable with the old structures and questioned Norman's claim to act on behalf of a new council whose powers exceeded those of the older councils. Some feared a dictatorial setup while others complained, 'This is not the mission I joined!'

Before committing Joan and myself to this position, I asked IC to consider afresh the necessity for one overall governing group and the Council produced a list of a dozen strong reasons which convinced me of their commitment both to the IC and to its officers. They made a significant addition to the IGS job description. To the original injunction 'To provide spiritual leadership throughout the Mission' (Appx to IC minutes, 1972) they added two key words, 'To provide spiritual and *authoritative* leadership throughout the Mission' (Appx to IC minutes, 1979).

Still I felt unsure. Would the new thrusts in outreach continue? Would fresh responsibilities divert Joan and me from our call to facilitate the preaching of the good news to people who had not heard? Or was God calling us to share the fire in our bones with the wider circle of the whole mission?

Early in the day on which I had to give an answer to IC, I came in my regular reading to Matthew's story of Jesus walking through the storm on Lake Galilee. He called Peter to the impossible, 'Come!' I read on, 'Peter got down and walked on the water to Jesus.' I reasoned, 'The task might be difficult but, if Jesus is calling us to it, he will enable us to handle impossible situations similar to Peter's.' After talking to Joan, I took the post, and she loyally shared the perplexities and pressures. In the difficult times afterwards I often came back to that passage, not only to the wonder of Peter walking on the troubled waters but to the second miracle: when faith failed, 'he saw the wind, was afraid and, beginning to sink, cried out, "Lord, save me!"' In times of failure the hand of Jesus would always be ready to reach out and rescue me.

*****

One of the questions that the leaders of AIM faced in the early seventies related to the continuing need for the Mission to exist at all. They asked, 'Did the multiplying churches in sub-Saharan Africa still require the help of missions from overseas? Surely the Holy Spirit, who so obviously resided in these believers, could enable them not only to manage their own affairs but also to evangelise the unreached peoples of Africa.'

African leaders answered the question. Among them, Bishop Ezekiel Birech told us, 'Our churches are strong but not mature;' they were strong in terms of numbers, but weak in understanding and applying the Word of God. Too few trained pastors served too many congregations. Referring to the average preacher in a congregation, another Kenyan complained, 'We cannot expect a cow to give good milk unless she feeds on good grass.' They implored the Mission to send more workers to develop leaders for the churches, not only in pastoral leadership but also in caring for community needs in the name of Christ.

My friend Pastor Peter insisted that the African missionary movement could not yet handle the unreached tribes. They needed to work alongside their western brethren.

Even with this encouragement, IC felt it should clarify priorities so that we focus on the real unmet needs of Africa. Delegates decided to bring all our ministry under the umbrella of one goal: 'to plant and develop maturing churches', and to add two priorities: 'through the evangelisation of unreached peoples and the effective development of leaders.'

To Joan and me God seemed to be clarifying the Mission's present ministries as well as stirring us to a fresh commitment for the new challenges which lay ahead. Convinced of the rightness of the IC vision, and supported by the strong affirmation of Council members, we embraced the changes with enthusiasm and set out to explain them to our members.

A missionary nurse felt discouraged. She said, 'I seem to spend all my time healing bodies but do little for souls.' As we talked I learnt that patients came from far afield, some from places where they never heard the gospel. In the wards they listened to a message from the hospital evangelist every day. They also saw a sermon in the nurse's loving care. Some responded, and returned to their remote homes with Christ in their hearts. Moreover she was training nurses. A student accompanying her could see the love of Christ in all she did. Regular Bible studies built upon this witness and laid spiritual foundations for the future ministry of these key young men and women. As she applied the mission goals to her nursing, this missionary discovered that she might be more fruitful than she had realised.

The IC produced policies which they expected our missionaries to implement. One stated, 'All ministry should be organised and operated so as to ensure its adequate national leadership and support as soon as possible' (IC Minute 9/ 79F). Although this might seem obvious, not all saw how it could apply to them.

I visited a secondary school to discuss the policy with our missionary teachers. I asked, 'When do you think you can expect an African Principal? How long will it take to have a majority of Africans on the staff?' They thought it would take a very long time, so long that they could not at present plan for it.

Similarly in a church hospital, the missionary doctor doubted if an African could take charge for many years. When I pointed out that African doctors administered the country's health programme and their specialists ran the departments of the national teaching hospital, his wife insisted, 'That couldn't happen in our hospital.'

I found people resistant to principles and policies which seemed firmly rooted in God's will. Although IC had been operating for six years when the Council appointed me to the IGS post, many members still doubted the concept of a top council making decisions which affected their own ministries. As volunteers, missionaries rejoiced in discovering God's will for their lives through personal acquaintance with him. They found their financial support through their own contacts – either churches or friends. This system encouraged initiative, personal devotion and commitment to a task; but it also fostered independency. While welcoming pastoral leadership which listened and cared, it shunned prophetic leadership which directed. IC wanted both.

I heard of discontent. When I expected fellow members of IC to spring up and say that I was indeed implementing the Council's decisions, they remained silent. A respected elder circulated a letter branding the IC as dictatorial. Another thought I was the author of the new ideas and asked if the initials AIM stood for 'Anderson's Independent Mission'. The criticisms surprised me. I wondered why people wrote in such a way instead of coming to talk quietly with me, to understand my viewpoint, to offer counsel and prayer.

Before the IC meetings of 1981, the Chairman took me aside and told me about an article he had read in a leadership magazine which described an American minister who gained such a reputation as a pioneer church planter that he was invited to pastor a large congregation. He failed, for his gifts did not qualify him for the new task. I wondered, 'Should I have stuck to the outreach work alone instead of taking on this wider task as well?'

In the subsequent week of meetings, criticism buzzed around my head. What had become of all the affirmations of three years previously? I seriously considered resigning. After pondering the possibility throughout one sleepless night, I came in my daily readings to Ecclesiastes: 'There is a proper time and procedure for every matter, though a man's misery weighs heavily upon him' (8:6). The author's word of caution came with greater force as he seemed to sense my weight of 'misery'. His advice continued: 'As dead flies give perfume a bad smell, so a little folly outweighs wisdom and honour' (10:1). Even though I felt justified in asking to be set free from the IGS position, I had to ask myself, 'What was guiding me, God's will or personal pique?' One smelt of wisdom; the other of folly.

Then I read a few lines further down: 'If a ruler's anger rises against you, do not leave your post; calmness can lay great errors to rest' (10:4). Probably the writer referred to a royal ruler but my ruler was this IC which seemed angry. With a force I have seldom known in reading the Scriptures I felt God say, 'On no account leave your post.'

Afterwards I pondered the Chairman's story and concluded that, despite some unfair criticism, I needed to learn a lesson in leadership: style matters as much as substance. What I had attempted was right, the way I attempted it was rash.

Our outreach experience may indeed have hampered me in the new role of IGS. In a pioneer thrust you must establish a clear set of goals and drive towards them in determined faith, refusing to be put off by hindrances or setbacks. A childhood image often stuck in my mind. As a great treat my mother took me to Bertram Mills Circus in London. I watched enthralled as a man climbed on to a platform and took into his mouth an object attached to one end of a steel cable, the other end of which was fixed to the centre of the high roof. Then he launched himself across the vast auditorium in a wide swing, supported only by the grip of his jaw. The pioneer must do that: get the bit between the teeth and never let go!

Buoyed by the visions of IC, I had assumed the missionaries would embrace the Council's wise principles. I sank my teeth into them and ran with them, expecting others to do the same. But I was moving too fast. I was crusading when I should have been counselling. With a traditional organisation the leader who plans change must interact, listen to objections and quietly explain decisions. Before my personal storm broke about me I had met Ralph Winter, the American missiologist, and he told me, 'It's like changing the direction of a great liner. You must not suddenly swing the vessel but turn slowly, taking a wide arc of ocean over many miles.'

I decided to cultivate two styles of leadership – aggressive determination for pioneer outreach and patient persuasion for established situations.

*****

Pressure eased in the work. I found a less threatening way of approaching another policy statement which, though innocent on the surface, contained a radical heart: 'In contrast to reacting to the flow of events, the Mission's intent should be management by objectives' (Minute 9/78.A). This meant praying for guidance, then drawing up specific goals for ministry, working out plans and finally reviewing progress with a view to determining new goals and repeating the cycle. IC started the process by writing ten-year goals and asked the other councils to break these down to short-term objectives for their own work. The process should filter down to the level of individual missionaries.

Two sticks of dynamite threatened to blow this concept apart: individual guidance by God and individual responsibility to him. One senior member quoted Paul, 'I care very little if I am judged by you.... It is the Lord who judges me' (1 Cor. 4:3, 4). No-one need review his work because he was accountable only to the Lord! It sounded pious, but was not the whole story.

Still smarting from my lesson about style, I grasped another about accountability. If leader and led could agree in advance to a set of goals, then a review performed a year or two later would simply be an objective evaluation against previously-set standards, with the leader adopting the role of monitor rather than judge. As a kindly counsellor, committed both to God's glory in fruitfulness and to God's grace in failure, he would encourage his charge to recognise goals achieved as well as those missed. The leader would affirm the former and, together, they would seek remedies for the latter.

I asked the IC to arrange for my own evaluation. The Chairman requested help from a Management Consultant, who had assisted the Mission greatly through the process of change. They surprised me with five pages of questions based on my job description, implementation of the IC minutes and my performance as a manager. After reading my answers they invited me to discuss them in Toronto, Canada. It gave me my first opportunity to talk about my work with leaders who seemed basically sympathetic. Although the discussion was confidential, we circulated the lists of questions to IC delegates to assure them that the process had taken place and it had been thorough.

At the next Executive Officers' Meeting I stressed the value of this process and suggested they submit to something similar. They wanted the same forms, suitably modified to cover their responsibilities. As members of IC they had helped make decisions; now they wished to know how effectively they had carried them out. I asked each council to appoint a person to help. We adopted some criteria: make it a pastoral exercise; rely upon measurable criteria rather than general impressions; affirm success; acknowledge failure with a view to increasing effectiveness; keep results confidential.

All the officers approached the exercise with humility, and most reckoned their performance too negatively. Consequently we could assure them that they appeared to us much more effective than their self-assessment indicated. At the same time their self-evaluation forms usually revealed at least one real area of weakness which we could discuss and take steps to remedy. One leader had encountered resistance to the orientation plan introduced by IC. Another was taken aback to discover that his articles and letters were heavy and dull, which meant that few took time to read them. Several found the path of leadership lonely and welcomed an understanding ear.

I wished to repeat this process annually but, as the number of the officers was too great and the spread too wide, we had to settle for every two years. These leaders in turn reviewed the ministry of all their members at the end of each tour of duty.

As more people came to work with us in the International Office, I sat with each individual every six months to draw up goals together so we could see how they had got on next time round. Quietly the practice began to permeate throughout the Mission without detonating any dynamite.

*****

Some IC members graciously attributed my early leadership problems to the number and complexity of my responsibilities. The Council recognised the need for other officers – someone to direct the personnel programme, ensuring that all new missionaries focused on our major goals; another to hone their ministry skills; an officer to take on my responsibilities for new outreach, and an administrator to care for properties and finance. This concern resulted in some of our most able missionary leaders joining the international team.

I found an enormous relief in delegating large chunks of my own responsibilities to these officers. They did much more than share my workload. Together we formed a leadership team, meeting regularly to share our perplexities and to map out the path ahead. We all brought different gifts. One possessed an almost uncanny ability to discern the way Africans would react to our decisions. Another – a nurse with great administrative skills – contributed her woman's sensitivity to missionary feelings. A frank Australian helped us see to the heart of our problems. I leant on them heavily in such matters as finance where I knew I was weak. We came from different nationalities and had worked in a variety of missionary situations. Most important of all, we prayed together. We set aside our first half hour in the office each morning and one morning every month for intercession, and a weekend a year when our mission family throughout the world waited on God.

Although we travelled extensively in order to maintain contact with our widely scattered members in Africa and the sending countries, we always needed much discussion before and after the two yearly IC meetings. Our task was to prepare the agenda based on input from the different councils and from our previous IC meetings. We researched new items and circulated papers to delegates well in advance of the gatherings. Then, when the meetings were over, we combed the minutes and decided how to implement them through the different mission councils.

AIM works best with a participatory system of leadership. Every active member* votes for a delegate to the ruling body, IC. The IGS and his team work together to provide the executive service without which IC could not be effective. I had found myself accused (wrongly in my opinion) of becoming too autocratic, and I recognised the danger. On the other hand I feared the position summarised by an American preaching in London about the army officer who said, 'I aim to discover the direction my troops are taking and then run round to the front so I can lead them.' Only a good system of evaluation can afford the protection a leader needs.

*****

In August 1978 I moved into the International Office in Nairobi's city centre on a day that Kenya came to a standstill,

---

*Membership on 31/12/1998

On the Field	620
Home assignment	167
Home staff	112
Studying	19
Between assignments	33
Appointees	78
Retired	253
TOTAL	1282)

for President Jomo Kenyatta had just died. I remember visiting the office and then sitting in my car parked in the street in order to listen to the radio. We all waited to see if his Vice-President, Daniel arap Moi, would succeed in taking over peacefully. Long afterwards the media told us that swift action by a loyal Army Commander-in-Chief forestalled efforts to frustrate the constitutional process, ensuring a quiet transition.

I commuted between the set of offices downtown and a residence a few miles away, possessing five bedrooms, two lounges, a dining room and two bathrooms. I hated the office location with all its noise and the twice-daily battle against rush hour traffic, and I also felt we could not afford such an expensive location. So we split our home and moved the office into half of it. As our staff increased, the office became like the proverbial camel which, getting its nose inside its master's tent, steadily encroached until it forced its owner out. By that time another house became available, smaller but perfectly adequate for our personal needs for the next few years.

Initially I thought that an African location suited our mission's central office. We could maintain the feel of the continent, keep in touch with African friends, worship in Kenyan churches and form policies where the rubber hits the road. Without doubt we enjoyed many advantages. But we ran into misunderstanding.

At the end of 1979 we completed the handover of the direction of our work in Kenya to the AIC. All missionaries engaged in any sort of church work became AIC personnel. In future the Church would approve new missionaries, orientate, assign and care for them. Most of our people welcomed this move as evidence that this great denomination

163

had, by God's grace, come of age. They gladly submitted to African leadership. AIC leaders, pleased with such recognition, graciously invited us to assign one or two AIM workers to their office to assist in managing missionary matters. Some theorists glibly claimed that we had achieved the old goal of the 'euthanasia of mission'.

Our new office, about two miles from the AIC central office, appeared to negate this advance. Although we were all members, and some of us ordained ministers of AIC, we worked independently. We represented the international organisation of AIM which, far from diminishing, was actually growing in size and influence. On behalf of AIM we negotiated the assignments of our personnel to several large African denominations in different countries as well as to governments and other bodies. We responded to requests from these organisations which tallied with our goals and insisted on negotiating adequate housing and care. We engaged in many activities which had nothing to do with AIC Kenya. In fact, the International Office of AIM acted as an independent organisation.

Norman had foreseen this problem in 1972 and set up his office in Kampala, Uganda, where the AIM was not working at that time. Idi Amin's coup and subsequent bloody reign forced him out and he came to Nairobi, thinking it would be a temporary home.

In 1985 I asked IC, 'Should we once again seek a neutral base for our office where we would offend no-one?' The Council agreed. After considering many options in different countries we decided on Great Britain as the most sensible, and acquired property in Bristol.

Moving out of Africa changed our relationships with the churches. Church leaders already applied to many western organisations for project moneys and sometimes for workers. To treat AIM in the same way posed no problem. When our international officers visited their countries the leaders welcomed us as guests and realised that we would not trespass on their responsibilities.

*****

Had we known the clouds of criticism, misunderstanding and resentment which would hang darkly over us in our early years as IGS, Joan and I would have rejected the job as possibly the disciples might have hesitated to obey the Lord's command to climb into a boat and cross Lake Galilee if they had foreseen the storm ahead. Mark (in ch. 6:48) tells us that 'he saw the disciples straining at the oars because the wind was against them' and yet he waited until sometime after 3 am before striding through the storm to their relief. The Lord always watches us struggle with our afflictions, waits for them to accomplish his hidden purposes and then walks across the wastes to rescue us.

12

FAMILY

I shared a conference room with a missionary who was serving a central African tribe. Eight years previously he had started preaching to this remote tribe, which knew nothing of the gospel, with remarkable results: the language analysed and written, a church established and sending out its first missionary and a community developing in health and self-respect. Lying under our mosquito nets on a sultry African night I listened to his description of the work and marvelled. If ever I had met a model pioneer, this was him. He told me, 'I'm getting married,' and then asked, 'Do you think I'll have to change the way I live and work?'

My mind went back to my early bachelor life in Turkana. I had empathised with Paul when he said, 'Those who marry will face many troubles in this life, and I want to spare you this' (1 Cor. 7:28). Despite the loneliness, I had valued my freedom to devote myself to the challenge in hand without the added burden of family responsibilities. But the time came for me, as it had now arrived for this brother, when God chose to expand my solitary witness to the more powerful testimony of a Christian home.

I told him, 'Yes; it's a revolution!'

I read of an early pioneer in central Africa who asked his new wife to sign a statement that she would not hold him back in any way from the work he had been doing. But the 'one flesh' relationship is more than two colleagues linking so that together they can accomplish more than the two could achieve on their own. It affects them at the very core of their beings, changing them into a new unit for God's service, challenging them to discover new modes of ministry and to develop new styles of living.

*****

Back in 1975, when the call came to leave Turkana, Joan did not find it easy to move from her full ministry of translating Scripture and teaching women. Sometimes she felt like Abraham's wife, Sarah, who gave up a familiar place where she felt at ease with her way of life because God had told her husband to move to a remote, uncertain new sphere. After the warm fellowship of a dedicated team, Nairobi seemed impersonal. Desperately aware of the need for a supportive praying group, we often felt alone.

At first Joan accompanied me on most of my long journeys so that we could think and pray together about the challenges of new outreach. We found that the most effective way to get work started in a new area was to spend time there, finding opportunities and then drawing a new team together, remaining with them until the members felt established. As our pioneer teams multiplied, the Nairobi office demanded more of my time. Then, once we agreed that I should accept the IGS position, we could no longer manage the long periods away which had been so fruitful in the Comores and Sudan.

While I had plenty to keep me busy, Joan wondered what she should do between trips. God had called her to spread his Word in Africa and she could not bear to be idle. For the first time since she became a missionary she felt unfulfilled because her task was unclear. IC, among its many changes, had instructed me to ensure that every missionary received a job description and I had made a start by asking leaders to sit with each individual in order to bring together the leader's concept of the tasks to be accomplished with the member's own sense of calling, and to write them down in a clear statement. It occurred to me that I had never done this with my own wife, presuming – perhaps arrogantly – that she would simply do all she could to facilitate my own work. So we took time one evening to list her responsibilities in her own special role.

At the head of her list we wrote prayer, for we knew we could accomplish nothing without it. We must both work at prayer – individually and together, in private rooms and in public meetings, as we travelled along the road and wherever we stayed. The fire for taking the gospel to the unreached still burnt in our bones, but now it flared up in new ways, as we prepared the way for others and then interceded for them.

As 'Wife to the IGS' many of her duties paralleled my own: by providing a home where guests could pop in and by accompanying me on many visits to missionaries and conferences where her relaxed outgoing approach to people compensated for my own stiffer manner. Two-thirds of AIM members were women, and they often found it easier to tell Joan about their joys, problems and ideas than to tell me.

Not so easy to define was her support for me by challenging my thinking, questioning my decisions and sharing my difficulties. Later, when I phoned her from England after the difficult IC meeting in 1981, she sensed immediately that I was disturbed. Joan told me later that she thought, 'They've clipped his wings.' Although I was sensitive to the criticism, she probably felt it more on my behalf.

In addition to her role as Mrs IGS she wished to develop

some interesting opportunities of her own. So we wrote down 'Bible studies and prayer meetings'. Over the years she gathered several groups, each consisting of a dozen or so girls, to study the Bible – Japanese servants, seamstresses, secretaries on an office rooftop, waitresses in a downtown coffee house. Then she commenced prayer meetings, particularly for fellow missionaries.

One day she went into a local Christian school and enquired if they needed help in teaching. They welcomed her to teach Scripture and music. We listed this and discussed her desire to approach other schools. Soon she found more opportunities than she could fulfil herself and encouraged other Nairobi-based missionaries to take them up. In one secular school of nine hundred pupils, the head asked her to take the whole school for singing lessons in three immense classes, with freedom to teach whatever songs she wished. They often walked out of the hall at the end singing some hymn or chorus which hopefully continued to buzz around in their fertile minds for a long time. Joan discovered a fine Christian teacher and suggested they study the Bible together. Others joined them and some met Christ as Saviour for the first time.

We agreed that whenever the children came home Joan would delight in the priority of being a mum.

*****

During our early years in the IGS office, anxiety for the family often dogged us. Their schools seemed so far away, even though they spent their vacations with us. We questioned our long separations: 'Is it right? Do they not feel unloved?' When Helen committed some offence at her boarding school, the authorities disciplined her severely and sent a message to our office asking me to phone. My efficient secretary passed the request to us in Vancouver, Canada, where we were representing the Mission in meetings. The news devastated us. We felt perhaps we were responsible by being so far from Helen, and even asked ourselves, 'Should we leave the Mission and seek a job in UK where we could make a home for our children in their late teens?' We loved our work and felt that God was drawing us closer to himself in many ways, but we did not wish any sense of personal fulfilment to obstruct God's will if he chose to send us in a different direction.

Some parents have advised me, 'God comes first, family second and work third,' but I have never found it as straightforward as this. Service to God, family, mission, church, community and country is all part of one package labelled 'God's will'. We learned that if we determine to discover his plan in each situation, he reveals the priorities. In this crisis God seemed to answer, no; he had called us and we must trust him to care for our children while we sought to see them as much as possible.

Such trust never came easily, especially as we knew they found it hard to say goodbye. Mary and Helen exchanged the family atmosphere of Turi School in the Kenya highlands for a more rigidly disciplined girls' establishment in the south of England. I managed to join them for the first half-term break and we spent it with my sister, Jean, and her husband in their vicarage on the south coast. As we approached the school after three happy days of holiday Mary turned a tearful face to me and said, 'I hate school!' I think that was our hardest parting. Growing up through the teen years never made return to school easier for her. The British Government maintained their generous provision of school fees and air fares. But holidays were far too short. Whenever the jet from Nairobi dropped into the morning cloud over Heathrow, Mary would sense a mood of depression and gloom settle on her. On the first day back she sometimes vomited.

Mary never resented our missionary call which caused all this separation. Joan once said to her, 'We would not have chosen to send you to boarding school if we could have avoided it' and she found that remark helpful. Despite the disadvantages, they always valued the compensations of a home in Kenya: camping with us in the Turkana bush, swimming in the sparkling Indian Ocean while I worked in a local hospital, encountering a wide range of cultures and meeting our host of Christian friends from many countries.

While still at school Mary as the elder sister had to accept responsibility for the others during times of difficulty. She surprised us. Late one night Kenya Airways landed them at Heathrow Airport after all public transport had ceased running. Mary, aged sixteen, badgered the airline officials until they agreed to pay a taxi to run them forty miles to their school.

The teachers reacted to her maturity with ambivalence. One wrote in an end-of-term report, 'Mary has good leadership potential but she needs to learn to exercise it responsibly.' She must have learnt fast for the next term they appointed her Head Girl and they found they could depend upon her for three terms. But she experienced the leader's loneliness when she realised she was no longer one of the girls and yet not a member of staff. The day before Mary and others were due to leave school, high spirits carried the lasses away as they celebrated their impending departure by flinging the prefects into the swimming pool fully dressed. The staff blamed Mary and punished the whole school by cancelling the sports due to take place next day. As a result we picked up a rather dejected daughter, glad only to get away from a strict environment she had outgrown.

Joan and I praised God when each in turn went to university; but we wanted more than an academic education. We had always prayed that God would grant our children the priceless privilege of knowing him and his Son, the Lord Jesus. None was settled in their faith, and the issues in their lives were so remote from ours that they found discussion difficult when it turned to vital concerns.

Mary studied for her degree at the Cambridge College of Arts and Technology. A biography of a great Scottish preacher, Duncan Campbell, challenged her, and the ministry of a godly chaplain steadied her so much that the Christian Union asked her to be their leader. Our work required Joan and me to visit London from time to time, and we always tried to include a run to Cambridge for a precious visit.

A friend introduced Mary to the competitive world of advertising in Edinburgh's famous newspaper, *The Scotsman*. This forced her to define her own faith as she studied the Bible and interacted with others, both believers and unbelievers. Many colleagues rejected her beliefs but some were glad of a sympathetic ear when trouble struck them. A director, who came to chat about the shattering experience of his brother's suicide, said, 'I wish I had your faith.' Another, devastated by his father's death, came for a chat.

Despite these opportunities Mary felt restless. She would say, 'Dad, I work in such a dark world; do you think God has something better for me?' I could only answer, 'Maybe, but remember God places his stars in the darkest places.' God had given her a rich insight into the realities of missionary service, so it seemed second nature to consider work overseas. She attended a huge missionary convention in Utrecht hoping to find an answer, but returned unconvinced. For a time she toyed with the idea of attending a seminary in Canada.

Two events settled her indecision. Helen booked into the London Bible College for a year and needed financial help and, at the same time, Mary's firm offered her promotion with increased salary. Yes, God wanted her in mission, but in a supportive role. She began to assist others and also served for a while on the AIM Scottish Committee until the pressures of marriage and motherhood put fresh demands on her time.

Many years later, when Mary left her eldest daughter in school in Edinburgh for the first time, she found it hard to be separated for a few hours from the little lass. She told us, 'Then I realised how painful you found it to leave us in the care of others for many weeks.'

*****

Helen graduated from Cardiff University and took a job as a teacher in Mombasa. Our joy at having her living in Kenya became tinged with anxiety when she wrote to her mother saying, 'I no longer believe as you do.'

We responded at once by telling her that her decision made no difference to our relationship; we loved her just the same and would always welcome her in our home. Whenever Helen came, we assured her that we did not wish to pressurise her into coming to church with us. At family prayer time, I told her, 'Your mum and I are going to pray; you're welcome to stay, but feel free to leave if you wish.' We were glad when she stayed.

Coming just at that time of criticism of my role in the

Mission, the sense of failing as a father added to the pain. But we took it all to our unfailing Father and realised that no parents can ensure the ultimate salvation of their children. We try to model Christ: to listen, teach, and pray, but ultimately only God's grace can give them his life. Helen's definite decision against the faith in which she had been reared forced us into a deeper dependency on him to work this miracle. Joan shared her sorrow with the missionary ladies' prayer fellowship and they reacted with sensitive understanding, promising to cry to God on our daughter's behalf.

In May 1983 a letter from Helen surprised us with joy. She told us about a friend she had met in Mombasa. 'She ... had never really surrendered to the Lordship of Christ – too much of herself in control. I felt the same in many ways – and hadn't really given up running my own show. It's better to be hot or cold rather than lukewarm, but it's horrible to be cold and know that being hot is the true way. I really want to do God's will now and pray that he will help me. It's hard to put into words, but I feel so grateful to be given another chance – even though it was there all along.'

Helen felt the next step in God's will for her was baptism. We drove the three hundred miles to her school in Mombasa. On a clear, hot morning the pastor of her church plunged her beneath the water of the school swimming pool as a testimony to her deliverance from sin and unbelief. Her life moved in a radically new direction. After further study, including a year following in my footsteps at the London Bible College, she believed the Lord wished her to serve him among Muslims in Tanzania and joined AIM for ministry in Dar-es-Salaam.

Helen enjoyed working with the Africa Inland Church Tanzania, but sometimes felt thwarted in her desire to focus on Muslims. In the midst of ministry to children on the island of Zanzibar, she got to know an English agricultural economist working for the government. In the romantic setting of a palm-fringed beach by the Indian Ocean, Angus proposed.

Angus and Helen came to Scotland for their wedding on a blustery March morning in 1993. Although both longed to continue sharing Christ with Muslims, they realised that God first wanted them to establish their marriage. Helen resigned from AIM (after serving for five years) and they both found jobs, settling eventually into an enthusiastic, Spirit-filled church in Cambridge. God has given them two lovely children and now their waiting is drawing to a close as the Lord is directing them to the Middle East – with the flames of God's Word burning in their hearts.

*****

Donald suffered some alarming experiences in Sudan, although letters took so long to reach us that he was usually out of danger before we heard. He had completed a degree in Arabic and English at Leeds University and then taken a teaching job with the Sudanese Government in order to develop more fluency in his new language. Hundreds of miles north of Khartoum he settled into a secondary school on the bank of the Nile in a small town called Delgo. Malaria laid him low and then hepatitis. Donald spoke gratefully of the Muslim head of religious instruction giving him a precious bag of oranges, and Egyptian Coptic Christians who came to chat and sing choruses. At one stage he wondered if the doctor would send him home.

At the end of his year, Donald sought transport to Khartoum but his ticket to fly on Sudan Air was useless as all flights were fully booked. At the same time a petrol shortage cut down the number of buses. He wrote that he and a fellow teacher 'eventually persuaded a bus owner to sell us tickets for the roof of his bus. They put large roof racks on the roofs of the buses where all the luggage is loaded and lashed on. We perched on top of this for some thirty hours hanging on as tightly as possible. Shortly after leaving the Nile for the open desert we had a blowout and, as we were carrying no spare, had to wait for another vehicle. We lay out on the sand for three hours looking at a beautiful cloudless sky with its brilliant array of stars until another bus came along and leant us a spare.' After wrestling all next day with soft sand, they arrived in the capital in the evening 'burnt to a cinder. My head had the dazed, floating sensation you get from sunstroke and we were all dehydrated.' In Khartoum they ran into riots but they needed to arrange flights to London. 'We found we could walk through the crowds without difficulty, only twice being caught by tear gas.' After a few days the military announced a coup and the streets filled with half a million delighted Sudanese.

Before leaving the country for a few weeks in the UK, Donald met officials of an American relief and development agency called CARE who asked him to return with them. Back in Sudan, they sent him with two others to survey villages close to the Eritrean border. For two months we heard nothing from him, and were sufficiently anxious to ask the Nairobi office of CARE to send a fax to Khartoum asking for information. But Khartoum kept silent. At last a letter caught up with us in New York where we were attending an orientation course for new AIM personnel. We reacted with a confusing mix of horror and relief.

Donald's letter told us about his unforgettable twenty-third birthday. CARE had sent him and two others to survey villages close to the Eritrean border. 'Coming near the side of a hill bullets started to hit the front of the Landrover and we leapt/rolled out and lay flat while shots continued to whine off the car or kick up dust around us. ... Seven men and a girl all armed to the teeth ran up extremely excited and angry. They shoved us into the vehicle, which was badly hit and pouring water all over the sand, telling us to drive towards the border.' Within Eritrea the engine packed up so the captors hitched two camels to the Landrover and dragged it across a river to their town.

At one stage during the next ten days of captivity their guards insisted that the lads empty their pockets before leading them outside, anxiously wondering if they were about to face a firing squad. The tense moment passed and they returned to their hut to wait.

The Eritrean People's Liberation Front had arrested them because they thought they were spying. But the prisoners soon became an embarrassment because the Sudanese Government reacted to the kidnapping by arresting some EPLF personnel who worked in Sudan, offering to set them free only when their organisation returned the CARE workers. In the meantime the government, realising that the motive for the kidnap was probably to gain publicity for EPLF, insisted that no news of the kidnap be leaked to the media. The strategy worked and, after ten anxious days, their captors released them.

Donald told us, 'Anyway we are all unharmed – miraculously – as everyone who has seen the holes in the Landrover cannot imagine how we escaped.' No-one thought of offering counselling to the young men after their release. In fact, the British Consul who interviewed them said, 'It was a bad experience for you in some ways, but you must put it from your minds and get on with your work.'

Donald had prayed before, but his experiences in Sudan brought a deeper reality to his dependency on the Lord. After his release he said, 'I have been thanking God for my life ever since.'

Three weeks before his contract expired, America bombed Tripoli in Libya. Outraged by the attack on a close ally, the citizens of Khartoum once more took to the streets in angry demonstrations and Donald's American bosses decided to withdraw all the personnel they could spare. Donald returned to Britain for two years in the Manchester University School of Business Studies. Gradually faith deepened until he came to a crisis at a Spring Harvest convention when, like his sister Helen, he handed over control of his life to the Lord Jesus.

*****

Paul stuck with the noble path of celibacy so that he could give himself fully to the ministry. The path of marriage is no less noble, but the apostle was right in saying that we who marry 'face many troubles' which the single can avoid. Despite these trials, marriage for us has developed our discipleship, sharpened our service and inspired our intercessions. In addition, God has given a mature fellowship with three children and their spouses – all committed to the Lord Jesus Christ – and we now face the challenge of praying that six grandchildren will follow in their steps. We can say 'thank you' to the great apostle for wanting to spare us troubles, but, 'No; if we had to live our lives again, we'd marry!'

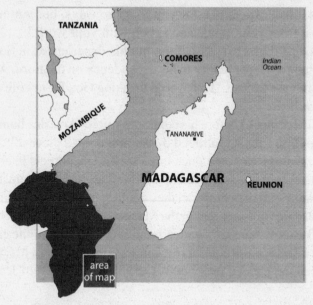

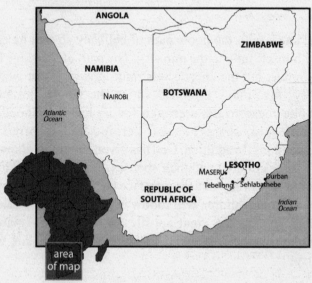

13

TEAMWORK

The Faith Mission in Bangor, Northern Ireland, was drawing to a close. I was to speak in the evening about Turkana, and in a couple of weeks we expected to fly to Kenya at the end of our home assignment. Spiritually I felt dry. For the last few days a longing for more of God had led me to look at many of the New Testament statements about the Holy Spirit, and now the preacher in the morning session was inviting people to visit him after the meeting if they wished to experience more. Normally I would rather run a mile than respond to that sort of invitation, but thirst forced me to seek him out and tell him of the drought in my soul.

The preacher challenged me, 'Can you think of any sin which is hindering the Holy Spirit in your life?'

My immediate reaction was, 'Of course not.' Then I pondered a problem. I faced a return to Africa with great reluctance because a colleague had criticised me grievously and I doubted if I could work with him again. I said to the Lord, 'That's his sin, not mine!' But the Lord seemed to reply, 'That's between him and me; he's my servant, not yours. I want to talk about your resentment against him.' So I saw my sin and, confessing it, believed God answered my prayer based on Jesus' promise, 'If a man is thirsty, let him come to me and drink. Whoever believes in me ... streams of living water will flow from him. By this he meant the Spirit....' I felt nothing new, but in the evening spoke with a fresh sense of God's presence. Returning to Africa I found my colleague had not changed – but I was different. Whenever I met him I quoted John 7:38 under my breath with the quiet prayer, 'Now do it Lord,' and love replaced all bitterness.

The experience of the Holy Spirit's power to transform relationships has upheld me on many occasions since. He has helped me in personal dealings with people who otherwise would have seemed obtuse and difficult. He has also given me a commitment to work with others of any organisation when I can do so without compromising in any sense my commitment to the truth of God's Bible and the reality of his offer of salvation in Christ.

Before commencing any outreach thrust Joan and I always asked ourselves, 'Is there anyone here who shares our concern for God's glory through the Gospel? ... Are there Bible believers who would encourage us to minister to the unreached? ... Would they assist us, work with us, or even sponsor us?'

Fresh ministries in four countries illustrate this concern.

Madagascar: who will work with us?

I met the General Secretary of the Bible Society of Madagascar when he visited Nairobi. He talked about a scheme for assisting some poor farmers. A landowner loaned the Bible Society 257 hectares in a lovely valley outside Tananarive, and Rev Jules Ramaroson settled three dozen Christians on it to earn a living. While some worked the land, others trekked long distances to evangelise and distribute Scriptures.

Jules told me about the sacrifices of the London Missionary Society workers when they arrived in 1818. With surprising speed they planted churches and translated and printed the New Testament. But a new Queen, jealous of the honour some of her subjects accorded to King Jesus, clamped down on the Christians, expelled their missionaries and ordered her soldiers to burn 'their Book'.

The Book survived and the persecuted church grew in hiding through three decades until the Queen died. The next Queen carried the Book in her hand during her coronation. An era of toleration arrived. New missionaries brought a new message which sowed seeds of doubt about the inerrancy of the Bible and turned out to be much more destructive than all the years of persecution. People crowded into the churches where they mingled their veneration of ancestral spirits with faith in Christ. A century and a half after the arrival of the first missionaries, Jules told us, 'We need the Gospel again for our churches are cold. Why don't you come and help us?'

When this respected church leader asked the Marxist Government for visas for two families, they agreed and for several years we worked closely with the Bible Society. Later, Colin and Christine Molyneux, our AIM pioneers in Madagascar, responded to a warm invitation to join Scripture Union, thus opening opportunities for preaching throughout the country and for developing key workers. A denomination, established to minister to the poorest of the poor, asked for our help in training their pastors. The International Fellowship of Evangelical Students welcomed a couple who had ministered in British universities.

None of these team situations functioned without strain but in each the Holy Spirit gave grace to work together.

Namibia: can two societies work as one?
This commitment to work with others took a new twist when we first approached Namibia. We shared our interest with

the Africa Evangelical Fellowship (AEF), a society similar to AIM which already had worked in the country. Three of their senior missionaries invited Jack Pienaar, our South African Director, and me to join them in an extensive trip. I wrote in my diary, 'By the end of ten days' travel a picture of mixed-up religion has formed in our minds. In one tribe a thin layer of Christian faith covers a tradition of immorality; in another, an elder leads worship in church on Sunday and at the ancestral spirits' fire during the week; elsewhere, Marxism and the gospel have become strange allies in the independence struggle.'

The AEF leaders told us that they lacked personnel. A semi-retired missionary lived in the capital, Windhoek, and a couple was away on home assignment. They asked, 'Why don't we work together?' Then looking at Jack they went on, 'We have no-one to lead this work. Could you possibly do it?'

We agreed that AEF would continue to administer the Namibian field. They invited Jack to join their International Council as he led the united team of more than thirty missionaries on behalf of AEF. After ten years Jack retired and the team wanted an AEF man to take over. Then AIM invited the new leader to join our IC.

As we were negotiating this joint team, I wrote to my opposite number, the International Director of AEF, and reminded him of Psalm 133, 'How good and pleasant it is when brothers live together in unity! ... For there the Lord commands the blessing, even life for evermore.'

Reunion: how can we overcome evil?
Joan and I became involved with AEF in a different situation – the island of Reunion. Finding this green, uninhabited dot

in the Indian Ocean 400 miles to the East of Madagascar, French sailors claimed it in 1642 and their settlers arrived twelve years later to cultivate sugar and coffee. They hired labourers in Indo-China and India and bought slaves from Africa. Chinese, Comorians and Malagasy added to a racial potpourri in a population of 650,000 crowded on to an island only forty miles long by thirty across. Mostly they valued their link with France. When a visiting politician told a political rally that they had chosen to become French, the crowd shouted him down, 'We were born French!' On one of our visits we discovered that their elected Deputy had become Prime Minister of France. With 40% unemployment, his constituents would expect much from him.

The expulsion of our missionaries from the Comoro Islands in 1978 precipitated our interest, for it meant that we had French-speaking missionaries who yearned for fresh outreach. Only one couple made it at first to the island. When Joan and I stayed in their little flat, they introduced us to an amazing religious medley.

Across the road from their home a staccato drum and tinkling bells called people to evening worship at the home of a nightwatchman whose ancestors came from Malabar in India. Today he is a priest. A litter of bananas, burnt leaves and candle stubs lying on the threshold of a gaudily-decorated shrine witnessed to yesterday's sacrifices to the 'trinity'. Above the entrance a huge heart, made of flowers, surrounded an *M* for Mary. Inside four idols sat gravely, two male and two female. We were told that one was Mary and another Joseph. The ladies each possessed two pairs of arms to demonstrate their power because, 'the gods of Reunion only have one set of arms and are weak; ours from Malabar are strong.' But that night the emphasis was on the priest's personal spirit who sat in another shrine waiting to be roused so that he could possess the priest. Some sick people waited patiently with their sacrificial goats and chickens, and a huge machete promised an orgy of blood. We rose and asked, 'What happens tomorrow?' The nightwatchman answered, 'Tomorrow is the big day. I will arouse Satan himself.' We departed disgusted and burdened to pray.

I was reared in a culture which derides such activities as meaningless, but local Christians are convinced of their power. Last year on the day of Satan worship, a child fell in the street and broke her neck. Many testify to the power of evil in this land. Long ago a mother cursed her children; now they hate their mother, even though she has recently come to know the liberating power of the Lord Jesus, and deeply regrets her folly for she knows that the curse had real potency. A lad engaged in occult practices became a Christian and fell in love with a fine girl. When she said she wished to delay the wedding, he picked up a hefty plank and battered her to death. He wept in prison as he wondered about the strange power which possessed him.

On my first visit, missionaries warned me that Satan attacks missionary families in Reunion. Later we remembered their caution and grieved when the marriage of one of our own precious couples fell apart, forcing them to withdraw.

Taking the good news of Jesus into a community where Satan has held sway for centuries invites vicious opposition. The Bible tells us to recognise the powers of spiritual evil arrayed against us and to resist them, armed with God's Word and our prayers for each other. In his great prayer for his disciples Jesus asks his father to 'protect them from the evil one' (John 17:15) and then goes on to ask, 'that all of them may be one, Father, just as you are in me and I am in you.

May they also be in us, that the world may believe that you have sent me' (John 17:21).

In a place where evil powers seemed rampant we saw that any suggestion of competition would play directly into our enemies' hands. We determined to work with our fellow missionaries of other societies under the discipline of the fledgling local churches.

I recalled a lesson from the Sudanese larder. Wild meat is a vital part of the diet in some parts of Africa. Obtaining it with simple weapons can involve real risk. In Sudan a Lokoro tribesman told me how they attack a buffalo. He explained, 'A man flings his spear and then lies down to tempt the animal, irritated by the pain of his wound, to gore him. While the beast is preparing to attack his first assailant, another lances him and flops onto the ground to invite the angry horns. Before the buffalo can decide which enemy to kill, a third spear impales him and he turns to see foe number three hit the dust ... and so on until he dies of multiple wounds. Then our whole village can feast.' I marvelled at their team work.

Lesotho: cooperation or compromise?
Working with anyone presents problems. I have shared a bedroom with many champion snorers, but my friend Dick was the champion of champions. Within five minutes of touching the pillow his trumpet strikes up, whether he lies on his back or his side or moves from position to position. Volume, pitch, beat and tune all vary. Maximal at the beginning of the night, it settles into long pauses in the small hours, and may disappear altogether by dawn. I moved my bed to the other end of the room but the music reverberated through the whole house. He lay down at 9.30. At first I went to bed at the same time with the idea of racing him into a

sleep which might be immune to noise, but he easily won the contest. Then I read until 11 pm in hopes that the main storm would pass by then.

I knew that together Dick and I must face greater tests to cooperation for the sake of Christ in the next few days.

In June 1986, the two of us arrived in the mountainous kingdom of Lesotho to negotiate a ministry for Dick and his wife, Barbara. Several years earlier the MAF had established a service, flying workers from the capital, Maseru, up into the heights of the Drakensberg range where snow blanketed villages for much of the year and, as the godly pilots quickly discovered, darkness covered the hearts of villagers. MAF asked AIM to join them in an effort to remedy this, and kept encouraging us during the next eight years.

We had learnt to view with caution statistics telling us that over 90% of the two million population professed to be Christian. We also wished to be sure that our emphasis on evangelising unreached peoples and developing leaders was really needed. After several surveys and much discussion with church and mission leaders, our IC, meeting in Nairobi, gave the go-ahead and I asked Dick to lead the new work.

I enjoyed getting to know him. We had once taken a safari together in Turkana (although I must have been a better sleeper in those days as I do not remember his nightly concerts), and since then I had followed his Theological Education by Extension (TEE) programme for AIC Kenya, which involved students working at home and meeting with a teacher visiting the area at regular intervals. As he had trained a Kenyan to lead the work, he and Barbara were free to move on.

At fifty-eight Dick trembled at the prospect of understanding a new culture and grasping a complex language. In our little room he said to me, 'I feel like a new missionary. I want to learn from whoever will teach me.'

We both had much to learn. We were entering a precarious ecclesiastical situation where we could easily go astray. On previous visits I had talked with high Anglicans, liberal Presbyterians, strongly reformed Christians, free Pentecostals, enthusiastic Evangelicals and others. In a major denomination the Seminary Principal held a feast to placate ancestral spirits whom he held responsible for a series of driving accidents although everyone knew he was drunk at the wheel! Many Christians found the politics of southern Africa more consuming than those of the kingdom of God. They had not realised that the first, though important, must be included in the second and subject to its King. On the other hand all these groups contained real believers. The question we faced was: can we team up with any without compromising our own principles?

I had previously met some of their missionaries who had wrestled with this problem. Two of them arrived at different conclusions.

Duncan, once a policeman during the Zimbabwean struggle, told me about his work for Scripture Union. When he came to Lesotho he reckoned he could best serve the churches by being neutral in his own affiliation. He soon realised that his acceptance by the Basotho churches depended upon his belonging to one. Although he found some of their practices strange to his evangelical Baptist ideas, he joined the Anglicans. As a white citizen of a southern African nation, he considered their commitment to peace and reconciliation more important than questions of baptism and liturgy.

The African Bishop welcomed him, loaned him a house and invited him into the Anglican schools. Duncan told me,

'I can put up with the tedium of genuflecting and crossing for the privilege of preaching in church and having access to the schools.' I recalled my own reaction against the formal Anglicanism of my youth and wondered how he coped with their beliefs. He reminded me that the faith of the Anglican prayer book is thoroughly biblical. He said, 'They feel threatened if I speak of being born-again or saved, but if I talk instead of exactly the same experience but call it commitment to Christ, they respond warmly.' Some other Christians had frightened them by their emphasis on immediate conversion through a decision of the moment which often did not stand the test of time. He went on, 'They do not dislike the reality of evangelical faith, but the approach.'

On that earlier visit, MAF flew me over massive mountains to Tebellong on the Orange River where Paul, a spry Swiss missionary doctor, met the plane and walked with us up a brown grassy slope to his home. He and his wife, Nellie, explained their personal spiritual odyssey. They had little idea of the gospel when they first arrived in Africa twenty years previously to work in a hospital belonging to a large Presbyterian denomination, the Lesotho Evangelical Church (LEC). 'Then the Lord met us,' they said and 'on our next leave we attended a Discipleship Training School organised by Youth With a Mission. Although we were old enough to be parents of most of the youngsters there, we entered right into the fellowship and were richly blessed.' Back in Tebellong they used the materials, which had so helped them, to teach twenty staff members. They discovered that 'for the first time we experienced real fellowship on our station'. With fine Christians now available, they instituted a community health programme in the mountain villages, including a healthy evangelistic element. Suddenly God was moving in the mountains.

A British pastor, accompanied by a church elder, visited for ten days of teaching during which he baptised five people, including the doctor and his wife.

Paul then wrote to the President of the LEC to explain his experience. He told him that he had discovered that believers' baptism was of fundamental importance and wished to continue the practice at Tebellong. The Executive Committee responded by forbidding him all spiritual activity and eventually asked him and his wife to leave. Later I learnt that, through the influence of a Baptist missionary who had served the church long ago, the denomination accepted those who preferred believers' immersion to infant baptism but, for Paul, this was a crusade to which the leaders responded in like spirit.

My heart warmed to both Duncan and Paul. I doubted whether in his determination to 'become all things to all men so that by all possible means I might save some' (1 Cor. 9:22), Duncan had compromised his faith. Certainly by humbly submitting to a situation in which he felt some discomfort, he had opened a door for effective ministry. Dear Paul, in his zealous stand for a truth over which Duncan could be flexible, had closed one which was wide open.

Dick too was expecting a door to swing open. We visited the LEC President's office. The President was out but we met three others, one a member of the Executive Committee. I outlined my previous discussion with the President about several staff needs including a TEE programme and presented Dick as the missionary we were offering. Dick told them what he had done in Kenya and the Committee member responded, 'For ten years we've been discussing TEE and have been unable to start.' The Principle of the Seminary said; 'We've prayed for years that God would send us someone who could develop TEE.' We arranged to meet the President three days later and, after prayer together, he told us that the Executive Committee had already discussed Dick's application and approved it.

For six years Dick trained many evangelists for the LEC until they came to a thorough understanding of the basic principles of salvation and the message of the Bible.

By 1995 the AIM team numbered thirteen. They invited Joan and me to attend their annual conference. Kathy, who was then leading the team, told us they had previously met in Durban but found that many tasks in the city shops drew some away from the meetings! So they decided to enjoy their fellowship together in a mountain tourist resort, Sehlabathebe. Approaching from South Africa, Joan and I anticipated a quick run along a good road to the centre. We soon discovered our error. For hours we climbed on rough gravel, sometimes twisting around high switchbacks where stones, dislodged by the Landrover wheels, tumbled down the mountainside. Joan wondered when she might follow them. Eventually we arrived at a small village possessing an airstrip where we were to await the arrival of the rest of the team by MAF plane. Kathy had arranged to hire horses to take them the rest of the journey but the owner had got the dates mixed up. Some set out to walk while the Landrover took a group of ladies on, returning two hours later to pick up the rest of us. Fortunately darkness concealed the hazards of the track.

At dawn, brilliant sunshine chased the mists away, revealing bare, grass-clad mountains which formed a basin with our little centre in the midst. A brook provided clear water. We could see no other house for miles and certainly no shop. We fed upon God's Word together and shared our needs for prayer. All spoke of their relationships with a local church or organisation. LEC had assigned two of our families to Tebellong – one couple, both doctors, was in charge of the hospital, and another pastored the local parish congregations. In the amazing goodness of God, they built upon the spiritual foundations laid by Paul and Nellie. Another couple had arrived not long before, to establish a team of nine in mountain villages where they were to learn Sesotho language and culture and seek to develop new congregations. They clearly recognised their first challenge: to train the team to work together in harmony.

14

TURKANA: PROGRESS
AND POVERTY

On July 1st 1994 our Kenya Airways Airbus touched down at Jomo Kenyatta airport as dawn was breaking over the Athi Plains to the East. A smiling man offered to carry us in his taxi wherever we wished to go. After discussing charges, Joan and I accepted his offer and he escorted us to the car park to climb into an ancient combi – dirty, rusty, with a starred windscreen and window absent on the driver's side – and we realised, 'Yes we're really back in Africa.' Cool morning air chilled us until the old thing heated in the laborious climb past the military hospital on the way to the mission guest house.

We planned to spend two months teaching in Turkana. The AIC Regional Church Council had asked us to conduct four seminars, at each of the main church centres, and for this we needed a vehicle. A good friend had promised to leave a car for us to collect at the AIM office. After resting a while, I walked round to pick it up in the afternoon. I expected a tough little Landrover and was surprised to discover a Subaru hatchback with over 200,000 kilometres on the dial. Mindful of our morning taxi, I wondered, 'Will this really carry us hundreds of miles on Turkana roads?' I had another question and asked my colleague in the office, 'Where can I load the large barrel of petrol I always need on long journeys around Turkana?' He laughed, 'Times have changed Dick.

You carry only a small can of spare petrol these days and fill up from the pumps in Lodwar.'

He was right; the changes amazed us. The gravel road north through mountains into the Turkana plains once took hours of patient grinding of gears, but now we found ourselves sweeping along tarmac at over 60 mph. We overtook huge articulated lorries laden with food for starving Turkana and drought-stricken Sudanese, traders' trucks supplying the shops and markets in the north, and swift vans, crammed with people and goods, racing to fit in as many trips as possible in twenty-four hours. As we entered Lodwar we ran past a radio station, which throws a directional beam upwards for airliners on their way to Nairobi, and then over a bridge where I once waited a week for the water to subside so I could cross the river.

The town hummed with people visiting the maze of sandy streets where grocers, bakers, butchers, fruiterers, bicycle repairers, newsagents, restaurateurs, inn keepers, tailors (including the Paris Boutique), tobacconists, shouting taxi-men, garages and two petrol stations plied their trades. The new government offices set up on their hill smartly proclaimed *Maendeleo* ('progress' in Turkana). Our friends, Wayne and Essie, were away but had invited us to use their home on the outskirts. Even here, on the edge of Lodwar, we could turn on a shower or switch on a light at almost any time of day. We received a phone call from an anxious father in USA enquiring about his missionary daughter, and we discovered we could, if we wished, dial direct to much of the world. Twenty years previously we had left Lodwar in the Middle Ages and now found ourselves thrust into the modern era.

We soon discovered that the church scene had changed

too. Some of the first Christians had developed into mature saints, widely respected in the churches and communities. They welcomed us to their homes and fed us with tasty meals. Maraka introduced us to her eldest son, employed by World Vision in the famine relief programme, and recently married to a Christian girl. Maraka told us about her own work in a vast refugee camp, mostly for Sudanese, eighty miles north of Lodwar. A couple invited us to their modern home for a delicious meal. He once helped Joan with her translation and, after our departure, had completed the whole Bible. Now they were planning to study in a Christian university in Nairobi in order to train illiterate Turkana to read it. A former Lokori Hospital nurse, who led the local Anglican Church, told us that Lodwar now had thirty churches where the Bible was honoured and its message of salvation preached – how different from my first visit with Tom Collins forty years earlier, when no church worshipped either in this town or elsewhere in the vast Turkana District.

We learnt strange lessons of grace. Many years ago we opened a small school in the south and installed teacher David from another tribe. He always left before the end of term and rarely re-opened school until two weeks after the starting date. Often he travelled the long distance from his school to Lokori complaining of sicknesses for which I could discover no signs. I never accused him of malingering but often thought it. Now, in Lodwar, I met the chairman of the pastors' fellowship who spoke glowingly of the teacher who had led him and others to Christ. 'Who was he?' I asked. He seemed surprised that I did not immediately recognise this supersaint and replied, 'Of course, he was David.'

A man who once professed conversion and worked closely with us went astray many years ago. Because of the education we had provided, the government gave him an important job. For years we grieved over him, his wives and concubines and eventually we despaired. Now we found his son in a leading position in Lodwar Church.

At Lokori I was asked to conduct a wedding. Thirty years previously I had married the bridegroom's parents in Lokori Church and soon afterwards helped at the delivery of their first son – the present bridegroom. At that time both worked in the hospital but the father was now a local chief. I talked to the young couple two days before the ceremony and discovered that both were fine Christians and she was one of the first graduates from the AIC secondary school for girls, close to Lokori Church. After the service the parents entertained three hundred guests to a feast supplied from his flocks and also from gardens resulting from the irrigation scheme we had initiated. Joan and I had been privileged to share in planting the seed of the gospel into what seemed very barren soil and now we could see fruit: an educated Christian family setting up home, a school producing lovely believers, fertile acres of farmland, grateful parents using their wealth to entertain guests.

*****

We knew of eighteen churches when we left Turkana in 1975. Returning after twenty years, we counted over a hundred congregations and our friends assured us that many more gathered in remote places. As we met the pastors of different denominations we realised that most owed their Christian beginnings to the AIC.

In Lodwar I was asked to preach on giving at a Sunday service which would include a Harambee designated for roofing the new church. Harambee really means 'Let's all push together' and is typically used when people crowd around a vehicle stuck in mud. Someone calls out *Harambeeee*, and on the *eeee* everyone shoves with all their might. Jomo Kenyatta, Kenya's first President, used it as an effective political slogan for uniting the new nation in the tasks ahead. The word acquired the special meaning of a fundraising gathering. We gathered within cement block walls, sheltered from the fierce sun by a huge tarpaulin. A good choir sang well, but continued for thirty minutes – creating a dullness difficult to shake off. Long intimations and a perfunctory pastor contributed no relief. Suddenly a poor Turkana woman rose and danced forward clapping her hands and singing locally-produced choruses in her own language, and the whole church came to life. At the end people crowded to the front – poor Turkanas with their few cents and wealthy government servants from other parts of Kenya with their hundred shilling notes – to make their contributions, and I sat in awe at such generosity.

Again the change amazed me. We had built the first church thirty years before with money from overseas, donated in memory of three missionaries who had recently died. So far as I knew, the only overseas contribution to this new building, three times the size of the first, would be Wayne's engineering skills in erecting the roof.

In the afternoon we were called to a Fellowship Meeting outside a church elder's house. Joan and I were offered chairs which we could just squeeze under the overhang of the palmleaf roof to find a slit of shade from the fierce afternoon sun. I had expected a dozen educated youngsters with their Bibles, but found a hundred folk of all ages singing Turkana songs with great abandon. A songster led off, 'Who made us?' and all responded, 'God made us.' Then he pulled on his nose and sang, 'Who made our noses?' and a hundred hands tweaked a hundred noses as they answered, 'God made our noses.' And so on for ears, lips, hair, hands until all collapsed in laughter.

The leading elder invited testimonies and several jumped up in rapid succession to announce 'Nimeokoka' (I am saved) and then mentioned some item for praise or prayer, usually finishing by leading off into another song in which everyone joined in, clapping their hands and swaying to the rhythm. Someone asked prayer for a blind woman. Another praised God for sending a friend to care for her home so she could attend the meeting. A woman in rags who needed to take a journey the next day requested prayer for her fare. Peter, a teacher friend of long ago, told of his son in a secondary school in another tribal area where 400 local lads threatened 100 boys from other tribes with such violence that the police closed the school. He said sadly, 'My son is due to write a key exam next Thursday and will miss the chance unless the school reopens.' People prayed with enthusiasm, taking up the various petitions.

No-one heeded time and I was glad, for I knew that the more we got towards evening before I had to stand up and preach, the more sting would have departed from the sun. When my turn came, I forgot the sun for joy of preaching to such a group.

The final act of worship was the collection. The elder urged us, 'Only three more shillings and a few cents to bring us up to 100 shillings.' When they reached 105/- (about £1.20), joy knew no bounds.

*****

We planned a five day seminar in each of four centres, primarily for pastors and evangelists. Sixty-two attended regularly, probably half of whom were AIC workers. On some occasions the numbers increased dramatically, notably when we invited wives to join us to consider what the Bible says about marriage and the family. We tried to limit our monologues to twenty minutes at a time, and interspersed many sessions when small groups tackled Bible passages with a list of questions for which they could find the answers.

Many were desperately poor. The African missionary in Kalokol, Ally, told me about a predecessor who had taken church money for himself. As a result the church had no cash to pay evangelists for seven months. Some left and joined other denominations. Those who plodded on in simple trust developed a tough dedication which made them a delight to teach.

Ally organised a Harambee, inviting friends from his home area in Kenya's fertile farmlands. Many came and gave generously to the support of these nearly-destitute evangelists. For a few months they received salaries; but the underlying problem persisted.

In one seminar the group wanted to talk about money. A desperately thin evangelist told us about the hardship he and his family faced on an uncertain wage of six hundred shillings a month (equalling £7.50). A kilo of sugar cost that man sixty of those shillings. If his child needed hospital treatment he would likely pay out another two hundred. He looked around the old church in which we were meeting and pointed to the new building alongside. He asked, 'Why build a new church? Surely this old building is adequate; should Christians not rather give to our salaries?'

Salary weighed heavily on their minds, and they often

looked to us for practical answers. Financial aid has flooded into drought-stricken northern Kenya and much of the economy depends on it. After government, the relief and development agencies provided most employment. Some have developed a system of child sponsorship in which they link a child with a specific overseas donor. Impoverished church workers wonder if a similar scheme could answer their own needs. One asked us, 'Can you not find sponsors for us in your own churches?'

Seeing their poverty, the question tore at our hearts. Surely we could assist. What is £7.50 a month to us – or even double that? But then, if we found sponsors overseas, when would the church find ways of supporting their own personnel? Would we not stifle such initiative as Ally displayed in organising his Harambee or the old-fashioned discipline of tithing? Could our giving actually hinder church development? We felt it best to leave the problem of salary to the African churches and to focus available funds on training in order to improve the effectiveness of God's servants, and to increase their potential for earning.

One man told us that he had carefully built up a flock of ninety-two goats over the years. Suddenly one night raiders swept down from Uganda and took them all. He said, 'Not long after, a visitor arrived and I had no food in the house. The only money was church collection which I had not yet passed to the treasurer. What should I do? Christian hospitality demands that I feed my guest, yet the only cash to buy food belongs to the church?' My own biblical answer would come from a background in which I have almost never lacked food, so I kept my mouth shut and left the answer to Africans who knew the pangs of hunger in their homes.

The evangelists wanted to discuss other matters beside

finance. The tribal practice of male initiation troubled them. Every self-respecting man passes through this; he cannot marry without it and certainly will never be recognised as an elder. Because Christians in other tribes had perceived much degradation in their own tribal rites, they had warned Turkana believers to renounce them and, in the past, the Turkana had tended to regard the ensuing shame in the eyes of unbelieving neighbours as part of the cost of following the Lord. Now they had reached a maturity which insisted on knowing if the ceremony was right or wrong in the light of God's Word. I opened the discussion by asking them, 'What do you see in it that the Bible would condemn?' Before we could continue, the pastor, who came from another area of Kenya, amazed us. He stood and announced, 'The Church Council has considered this matter and forbidden it.' He gave no reason and quoted no Scripture, simply stifling discussion. As a result the problem chuntered on for years.

Although tact forbade us from continuing that particular enquiry, we wanted the evangelists to realise that the Bible has light to shed on our problems if we but pose questions to it. Most of us, who have taught the Bible in Africa, have slipped into the error of giving our own Bible-based answers to people's problems rather than equipping them with the Bible-searching skills which can enable them to find their own solutions.

An obstacle to understanding God's truth is language. The language of communication in the Turkana churches was mainly Swahili. Missionaries (including ourselves) were much more comfortable in using this trade language than Turkana. Initially the only Bible available was in Swahili, and much of it was beyond the comprehension of people possessing very limited education. We urged them to use the increasing number of books now translated into Turkana, but they showed a strange reluctance, possibly reckoning that somehow their own language was inferior. We were astounded. We had spent years struggling to learn Turkana so we could share the gospel with as many Turkana people as possible, and here were evangelists who spoke it perfectly and yet insisted on using a language which they only partly knew and which certainly passed over the heads of many of their hearers. In our seminars we asked that, as far as possible, our readings come from Turkana Scriptures even if we referred to the Swahili text as well.

The Kalokol group convinced us of the rightness of this policy as we saw the impact of the Scripture in their own language.

Arriving at this centre beside the huge Lake Turkana, Joan and I set our beds on the verandah of the little guest house in order to escape the fierce heat and to benefit from any cooling breeze. We had forgotten the sandstorms that come sweeping across the desert. Sheets, pulled up around our heads, provided little protection from the howling gale, so we rose at dawn with sand filling our beds and plastering our faces.

We wondered if any evangelists would show up for the classes, but they came, leaning into the wind and rubbing grit from their eyes. We had brought enough copies of the most recent Bible Society publication, *Ngieosio* (Psalms), to give to each participant. Joan chose to teach some of these to the group. She asked one-armed Lorus (a crocodile had taken his other arm) to read Psalm 63. He reached verse ten and read, '*eario kesi a ngakwaras, toliworos akimuj a ngikolowoi*' ('They will be given over to the sword and become food for jackals'). The class gasped at the earthy reality of their own language. Hitherto they had tried to read the Psalms in the trade language, Swahili, and never understood them. Now they heard God speaking directly to hearts disturbed by struggles, temptations, loss, poverty, disease and injustice.

Later we returned to Lodwar for the official presentation of the new little volume by the Bible Society of Kenya. People from many churches gathered in a clearing under tall acacias at the river's edge. Joan glanced up and nudged a friend beside her, 'We've other guests,' she said, and pointed to baboons swinging in the treetops. The Secretary of the Bible Society spoke and then he introduced the first translator of the Bible into Turkana, none other than Joan. So they all demanded that the Mother of Mary climb on to the shaky platform to greet them. We sang and preached and praised God for all his goodness.

*****

When I first visited Lokichogio on the Sudanese border in 1957, it consisted of seasonal wells in a river bed (so deep as to require ten women to raise a bucket of water) and Kenya's remotest police station, set close to three mountains. Lush vegetation attracted the Turkana herds and these in turn tempted raiding parties to cross the border. Now a town had grown up dedicated to famine relief in Sudan. Forty agencies provided homes, offices, stores and often a workshop for their expatriate personnel, and employed a host of local workers. A clutch of shops nestled alongside one of the busiest runways in Kenya. At first light huge aircraft woke us as they flew northwards laden with food and returned with patients for a temporary four hundred-bed hospital run by the Red Cross. Our twelve disciples suffered a little from the six hours of unaccustomed study, punctuated repeatedly by the thunder of an airliner shaking the church and silencing the teachers.

Weeks of teaching in the four centres made us glad to tumble into our beds on the final Friday evening, but we had reckoned without another aspect of modern living – the disco. The thump began at the local hotel as soon as our heads sank into the pillows and continued until 4 am. Saturday night treated us to the same noise and left us like rags for the two services next day – one in English and the second a two hour marathon in Swahili interpreted into Turkana, which appealed to the educated but passed above the heads of ladies sitting in their goatskin clothing.

We left Lokichogio and pondered the worship services in which we had taken part over the last two months. The Turkana are boisterous people who delight in vigorous interaction and turn every discussion into a drama. They have already produced an impressive array of their own hymns. The liveliest congregations we saw were led by Turkana, using their own language and inviting all to take part. The evangelist, living close to the people and not yet educated into other church traditions, is the key to worship and growth. We felt the greatest missionary challenge is to develop Bible knowledge in these precious men and women so that they can grasp its relevance to their own lives and pass it on to others.

We ran southwards delighting in magnificent views of the mountainous Ugandan border, all dusted on the Turkana side with fresh grass from recent rains. Dark clouds threatened to fill the rivers ahead of us and made us anxious about the final crossing just north of Lodwar. Lines of stationary vehicles on both banks showed that our fears were well-founded. We took our place in the line and walked to the concrete drift to assess the water level and saw, a few yards downstream, a forlorn Landrover on its side. Fellow travellers told us that Somali traders, high on their drug miraa, had attempted to cross the previous night without first measuring the depth and strength of the flow, and they had all been swept from the ramp. Our informants added, 'The river ate their car and all their goods.'

After two hours waiting, the river dropped a few inches and a big lorry lumbered across, creating a huge wash. Others, all of them larger than us, followed. I still felt the level was too high for comfort but the sun was setting and we did not want to sleep beside the river. Just in case we should have the same experience as the Landrover, I took Joan's hand and led her across on foot, feeling the strength of the river clutching at our knees. Then I returned to the Subaru and, with my heart in my mouth, nosed it into the stream while Joan prayed. It crept over with water surging above its wheels, climbed the far bank and stopped, dripping like a champion swimmer as if to say, 'Why did you ever doubt me?'

*****

Sickness appalled us throughout our stay. Chest infections and malaria devastated many families, particularly the little children. A grateful ex-patient invited us to her home for a meal and told us both about the illness which carried off her small daughter the previous year, and how she and her evangelist husband rejoiced when their son completed secondary school a few months later. 'Surely now,' they said to each other, 'God will get him a job and relieve our chronic poverty.' An epidemic of jaundice broke out. The lad developed a fever, became yellow and died.

Then Atabo arrived, brought by her mother. We had known

her as a small girl at Lokori but were shocked to see her as an emaciated woman in her mid-twenties. We took her to the hospital for tests and they diagnosed AIDS. The mother told us Atabo had gone off with a policeman who subsequently deserted her but took all her children, leaving her with the lethal legacy. A few days later she died.

Our hostess, Essie, spent much time visiting patients in the local hospital. Pastor Paul from Lokichogio was brought in suffering, so he was told, from typhoid. As she sat at his bedside day by day, Essie, herself an experienced nurse, became unsure about the diagnosis. Seeing a senior looking visitor on the ward wearing a white coat and carrying a stethoscope, she asked, 'Could I trouble you please to examine this man?' He agreed and then said, 'This man has ruptured his appendix and is developing peritonitis. Without an operation in the next few hours he will die.' He went on to explain that he himself was a throat specialist visiting with some students. He added, 'There's no-one here who can perform this operation.'

Essie knew of a Red Cross surgeon in Lokichogio. She telephoned her nurse colleague there and asked her to enquire if this man would accept the pastor as a patient in his hospital although it was set apart for Sudanese patients. When he agreed, she and Wayne drove him the 150 miles and found the surgeon with his operating theatre ready. Pastor Paul survived.

Another missionary nurse, Renate, showed us round the Health Centre where she had begun work years before. She carefully nurtured some Christian youngsters, shepherding them through high school and often helping with school fees. When they came home in the vacations, she welcomed them. Renate sent some for nurse training and trained others herself so that shortly after our visit, the Turkana staff could run the Centre, with Renate keeping her eye on the finances and looking forward to soon handing on that responsibility as well.

Renate promised to help Lokori too. After our own departure from Lokori, no doctor could be found to replace us and the hospital was downgraded to a Health Centre in the care of missionary nurses. Eventually the supply of nurses dried up and it took another step down as the AIC requested the government to take on the responsibility. The place was closed except for three rooms for outpatients. Thieves helped themselves to mattresses and bedding and the facilities deteriorated.

The African missionary pastor in charge spoke about his longing to return the Health Centre to the AIC. I told him that I felt the answer to their invitation was to develop a Centre along the lines of Renate's at Lokichogio, with well-qualified local people in charge. 'If you do succeed in finding missionaries to run it again, they will eventually leave and the place will collapse.' One of the evangelists shared with me his ambition to train as a Community Health Nurse and I encouraged him. Four years later he returned to lead the work under the skilled but distant care of Renate and the Government was glad to give it back to the AIC. We still pray for a doctor to assist all the AIC health care throughout Turkana but without disturbing the Turkana management.

Towards the end of our seminar week at Lokori, the Pastor asked me to join a meeting of chiefs, councillors and tribal elders in the church. One started by saying, 'Your coming is like the clouds which herald the blessing of rain.' Another told me, 'People way down the river have heard that *Keyangak* has returned.' (*Keyangak* means 'Take a deep breath', my

Turkana name because I so often used the word to patients as I rested my stethoscope on their chests.) The meeting had been called to beg us to settle among them again. The local chief said, 'We have 40,000 people in the District and not a doctor among us. The nearest is a hundred miles away in Lodwar.' The father of the bridegroom whose wedding I conducted ended his little speech in tears. He promised, 'If you come back I'll resign my position as chief and come and work for you again in the hospital.' After three hours my heart was really torn, but I had to tell them, 'You need someone younger, and really you need a Turkana.'

With that sad note we turned south again, this time towards Nairobi. The Subaru seemed to fly up the mountain pass into the cool highlands and then down the long road to the capital. It had given just one problem throughout the whole trip – a puncture. As we returned it to the mission office, we felt we were saying goodbye to a faithful friend.

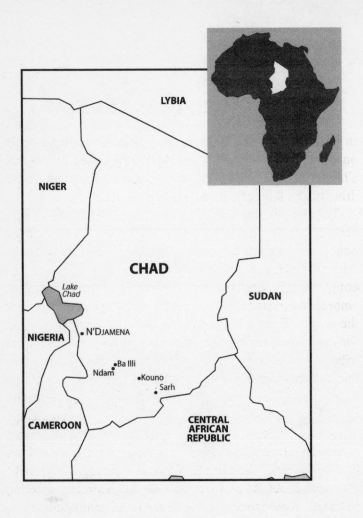

15

CHAD: FAITHFUL IN THE FIRE

In 1986, before our expulsion from Sudan, I visited a camp on the western border where ACROSS cared for 18,000 Chadian refugees. My heart went out to people running from drought and danger into even greater destitution.

Throughout the seventies and early eighties, drought, accompanied by its black horse of starvation, hammered the Sahel countries which stretch westwards across the bulge of Africa from Chad. Concerned missions sent delegates to a conference in England and noticed that these countries embraced a mass of people groups who were also starved of the gospel. Even though missionaries had worked in Chad for many decades, no-one knew the number or location of tribes in Chad who suffered this double deprivation. My friend, Maurice Wheatley, attended that meeting in his capacity as UK Director of AIM and sent me a report with the suggestion that our mission might take up this challenge.

News of tribes anywhere who had never heard the gospel always filled me with a restless, almost painful, unease. I felt Paul's shudder, 'Woe to me if I do not preach the gospel.' But what about the missions and churches already working in Chad? Would they want us or see us as competitors?

I wrote to several leaders. Without exception they responded warmly. A prominent Chadian, Rene Daidanso, wrote that it would be 'good for another mission to evangelise the north because the country is so large'. In view of the tough terrain and tense political turmoil, he cautioned, 'But it needs special missionaries.' Patrick Johnstone, author of

Operation World, spoke for his mission, 'There is an enormous amount to do, and WEC would welcome AIM's involvement.' One of the larger groups, The Evangelical Alliance Mission (TEAM), offered to sponsor and assist us. Thomas Kaye, the President of the Eglise Evangelique au Tchad (EET), shared with me his own longing to send the message of God to these tribes but added, 'We cannot do it alone yet; we need to work hand in hand with you.'

I asked two experienced missionaries, Les Harris and Dr John Marcus, to visit and find out if Christians there would welcome another society. In January 1984 they spent ten days in the south and centre and sent a positive report. They concluded, 'We could see first hand the needs of some 2,000,000 who have scarcely had contact with the gospel.' Like Daidanso they stressed the need for special people, 'Only a candidate with deep conviction would be able to withstand the heat, sand, political uncertainties, Islamic pressures and eventually the problem of schooling for their children.'

We needed more detailed information. How many tribes were we thinking about? Where did they live? Were they nomads or settled pastoralists? What religion did they follow and how diligently? Did they know anything of Christ? Could they read? Which of their languages possessed any Scriptures? What needs did they express for health care, education, water supplies, agricultural assistance, veterinary care or anything else? I shared these questions and many others with two New Zealanders, Ben and Winsome Webster, who had already worked with us in Kenya and Sudan. They agreed to attempt a survey of the whole country, taking as many months as needed to get a clearer picture. First they must learn French – no mean task for a couple in their sixties.

Early in 1987 they told us they felt ready. But in our office we received news which made us hesitate. Since independence Chad had known twenty-five years of turmoil punctuated by outbreaks of vicious civil war. At that moment fighting was again escalating. Should we send our missionaries into danger? Perhaps they ought to delay? But they told us, 'We believe God wants us in Chad. We are not getting any younger. Please may we go?' They went and never encountered any gunfire, bombs or landmines.

Three years later I joined them for a memorable fortnight – my first in Chad. We spent a weekend in N'djamena, the capital, and saw the signs of devastation when years of war resulted in 95% of the population fleeing the city. The main tarmac roads ran between stone-walled buildings, often roofless and pockmarked by bullets. Old vehicles and bicycles circled around potholes in back streets, where high walls and iron gates hid the homes of the wealthy. Poorer sections pulsated with people on foot. Religion split the city. On Fridays Muslims in the northern locations prostrated themselves in mosques; while on Sundays thousands in the southern districts crowded into churches.

Some acts of God awed me as I met missionaries already established. Erika and Marguerite ran an orphanage close to the Sudanese border. When Libyans advanced from the north, French airmen offered to fly them to safety. They asked, 'May we bring the children?' A firm 'No' persuaded them to remain. The hostile army engulfed them and for a while left them undisturbed. But they found feeding the children hard. Having bartered their furniture for food, they began selling sheets of corrugated iron from the roof, followed by the trusses. As Christmas approached Erika asked the Lord for some special treats. Marguerite thought she was going too far when she even listed the menu! A few days before the celebration, the Libyan Commander visited to discover who they were. He accused them, 'You're receiving money from America aren't you?' They laughed and, pointing to the roof, told him how they bought food. Next day a Libyan army lorry drove up with a load of staples including rice. Then a carton arrived containing apples, oranges and cheese – three of the items on Erika's Christmas prayer list. The Commander called again to explain. 'When I told my men how you obtained food,' he said, 'they collected money to buy these gifts for the orphanage.' For a year war cut off the outside world but the Lord took care of them and their charges.

Other stories shocked me. An early President, Tombalbaye, tried to return people to their cultural roots by insisting they renew initiation ceremonies which Chadian Christians regarded as too vile to perform. Some compromised, but many stood firm to their convictions. Three hundred deaths were reported. I heard of pastors who were buried up to their necks and left to die in the blazing sun, and of people taken to lonely places and shot. When missionaries of one society complained, the authorities expelled twenty-two of their members.

On my fourth day we drove through N'djamena towards the single-lane bridge over the wide Chari River. We just managed to squeeze on to the bridge around a huge lorry which had smashed through the railings. The cab hung dangerously over the water, prevented from falling only by the weight of its loaded trailer. By evening Ben and Winsome brought me to their base in the small town of Ba Illi and introduced me to the two missionary nurses who joined them in their extensive survey trips. They all lived in simple homes, built from sun-dried bricks and rented from local people for £8 a month. The blazing sun, beating on their iron roof, drove the daytime temperature so high that we used the bedrooms only at night. During the days they entertained visitors in an open-sided shack, covered in palm fronds. A woman brought water on her head while another took our laundry to the river. At night we tasted the luxury of electric light, generated by a roof panel using Chad's most abundant asset – sunshine.

The Eglise Evangelique assigned a pastor, Philemon, to the team. Master of six languages and possessing an easy-going friendliness, he provided the key to their relationships and the channel for most of their information. Christians from the south had moved into this predominantly Muslim area and set up their little church, focusing on their own community. Their pastor, Pierre, welcomed us warmly and took us to see an extensive church plot on which he hoped we would build the schools and hospital he had seen on mission stations elsewhere. As a token of the community's interest, the Christians had already produced six thousand bricks and dried them in the sun. I asked him, 'Where will you find Chadians to staff this work?' He replied, 'Missionaries will help us.' I countered, 'But what if they have to leave?' He paused and then answered, 'Well ... then we will manage as best we can.' I felt uneasy.

We drove on several hours to Chad's third largest town, Sarh. A group of Christians had arrived here several years previously and joined a church. But, wishing to worship in their own language, Ngambai, they commenced a prayer cell which expanded until they felt justified in asking the Central Church Council to assign them a pastor. Etienne arrived four years before my visit and, under his leadership, the congregation had swollen to 600 and had planted six daughter churches. One of the church elders was chief designer at the local textile factory. He informed me that the Pope planned to visit Sarh at the end of the month. The government had ordered two million metres of cloth printed with pictures of the Pontiff and the President so that the whole population might turn out dressed and shirted for the three hour visit.

Ben and Winsome told me that, on their first safari to one of the six daughter churches, they looked for a place to spend the night. Their vehicle disturbed oxen drawing a cart. When they asked for directions to the church, the driver replied, 'I'm an evangelist. Come and stay with me.' He became a firm friend. So now, wanting to contact the Ndam people, we went to ask him the way. This vigorous young man treated us to beakers of tea and then, wheeling out his motorbike, bumped down a scarcely visible track ahead of us for twenty kilometres. By then the road was clearer and he felt able to leave us. We crawled along, sometimes diverting round the bushes, often crashing over them, to meet another missionary evangelist called Gabriel. He lavished hospitality on us as African Christians, even the poorest, always do.

Gabriel told us that, at the end of the nineteenth century, Sudanese invaders insisted that people convert to Islam. They ruthlessly killed any who resisted, even mixing blood with the mud of their bricks. Although they said, 'A religion that has to use the sword to convert people can't be much good,' the people still remained loyal to Islam. A church, commenced in the mid-sixties, collapsed under the Tombalbaye persecution and never got going again. When I asked Gabriel how many Christians remained, he replied, 'I only know one.'

The Ndam church would not be reborn without cost. A few months after our visit, Gabriel was riding his bicycle when a man stopped him at gunpoint, took all he had and then shot him through the chest.

We drove on for several days, dropping in on churches,

clinics and a Bible School in an area obviously well evangelised. Our final goal was a conference of TEAM missionaries. People were asked to share their experiences. Several wept. Service in Chad is hard. They faced loneliness, frustrations, discouragements and sometimes danger.

A French missionary, Charlotte, worked in Bebalem, a big hospital belonging to EET in the well-churched south-west. Due for leave several months before the conference, she felt so discouraged that she had almost decided not to return. Because a handicapped lady needed help in her flight to Paris, Charlotte agreed to advance her flight by a week. Seven days later a bomb destroyed the UTA plane on which she would have travelled. While grieving over those who died, she suddenly realised that God had spared her life so she could continue to serve him in Chad.

Ben reported on his three years of survey. 'I have tried to make a list of the 181 peoples in Chad ... as well as the 135 languages they speak.' An astonishing 115 lacked any church and could count on no more than a dozen missionaries. He went on: 'We have only just begun. We need to follow up with more detailed research in order to draw up an overall strategy for the whole country.' We discussed the beginnings of this strategy. Then I flew back to N'djamena with MAF while Ben and Winsome prepared for another sweep through a vast area they had not visited. Relaxing high above the brown, scorched countryside, I compared the Websters with Joshua when the Lord told him, 'You are very old and well advanced in years, and there are still very large areas to be taken over.' Then God listed them with the details of all their peoples.

Ten years later, long after the Websters had retired, I returned to see how others had tackled their list.

*****

Air France touched down before dawn in November, 1998. After struggling with a pestering porter and an acquisitive customs officer, I was pleased to see the tall figure of John Marcus striding towards me. He took me to his home in N'djamena for breakfast. Following his exploratory visit to Chad in 1984, John had returned to Zaire (now the Congo) where he continued to organise the health care programme of our large partner denomination. He aimed to develop a scheme and train national workers so that they could run it eventually without missionary help. Nine years later he and his wife, Beate, moved to Ba Illi in Chad where they worked for three years before taking up their position as Team Leaders. As he drove me to Ba Illi, he told me about their early days in Chad.

No medical facility existed in this town to care for its 5,000 people. Pastor Pierre and his elders expected the doctor to set up a new health centre and become the pivot at its heart. John determined that the venture would be Chadian from its inception. He asked the denominational leaders to assign an *Infirmier*, trained for two years in Bible School followed by four in Bebalem Hospital. They sent Paul and immediately John invited him to take charge. Wanting to avoid heavy dependence on expatriates, John resisted community pressures to run a daily clinic, preferring to leave it to Paul, with himself available to give advice only when Paul asked. When John moved to N'djamena three years later, Paul was firmly established as the skilled and caring provider of health care.

From N'djamena John monitored the building project to its completion. Now we were visiting Ba Illi to take part in the official opening of the new centre. I slept in the little guest room, several degrees cooler than any other room on the compound because a large tree sheltered the iron roof from the fierceness of the afternoon sun. Even so the night started badly. Cocks crowed (even at midnight), donkeys brayed, crickets chirped, drums throbbed, neighbours sang and dogs barked until about 2 am, after which I dropped into a sound sleep.

Civic and church leaders had already gathered when we reached the new buildings next morning. Many Muslims in the crowd obviously welcomed this new project warmly. The leaders invited John to speak, and he reminded them that the townspeople provided much of the labour and the bricks for buildings while the evangelical agency, Tear Fund, assisted with finance to launch the project. After several speeches Paul led us through the buildings – two rows of rooms strung out on opposite sides of a square, small but adequate and, most important of all: their own!

I noticed several staff working with Paul and wondered how the church found money to pay these employees as well as to fund medicines. John explained, 'Yes; we helped find finance from overseas for some of the building expenses, but for running costs the centre is self-supporting. Paul sets the fees and all the staff ensure that people pay.' I knew that in many health care programmes (sadly those run by churches as well as governments), staff are tempted to pocket money or to sell drugs for personal gain. 'We don't have that problem,' John told me; 'Firstly we try to employ Christians. Then, each employee knows that his or her salary depends on the honesty of all. Finally, if a person is tempted to help himself, he realises the others will soon become aware of his dishonesty.'

We encountered the same insistence on local leadership at the Missionary Training Centre where I met a middle-aged

221

couple, Moise and Catherine Baou. Initially Ben Webster had urged AIM to find an experienced missionary to head up this programme, but no-one offered. Moise was pastoring a congregation of a thousand in the EET heartland. When he heard of the new venture, he felt God leading him to train missionaries. Moise applied for release from his pastorate so that he could study in the AIC Missionary College in Kenya. He learnt English, persevered through the fifteen month long missionary course and then accepted the EET appointment to pioneer their new missionary centre. By that time Janny van der Klis, a veteran with considerable experience in Turkana and Namibia, had agreed to a request from AIM's Team Leader that she assist the Pastor. When I met Moise, another Chadian had replaced Janny. He told me, 'I hope to study missions in a Nigerian Missionary College and to return.' Moise took me to meet the thirteen students, all of whom had already graduated from Bible College and gained some pastoral experience. Moise said, 'Since we commenced four years ago, twenty-seven couples have passed through our course and all but two are now working among unreached tribes.'

We called at the home of one of the graduates outside Ba Illi. Janny told me his story. Musa belonged to the Kwong tribe, but grew up with his Muslim uncle in another area, where he too followed Islam. When the troubles of the Tombalbaye era broke out he was forced to return to his parents' home. The good news of Christ had recently reached the Kwong and Musa responded from his heart. As a young Christian he developed a concern for members of the nomadic Mbororo people he occasionally met as they passed through his area. Several became believers, including a chief and his nephew. Wisely he realised his need for training to equip him for ministry to people of a different culture and came to Ba Illi. His Mbororo friends often visited him at the Missionary Training Centre where they got to know Moise as well as other pastors. The chief thought he must learn to read before he could join the church but the pastors told him, 'No, you must simply confess your sin and turn from it to Jesus, believing him to be your Saviour.' They agreed to baptise the chief and two others in the Ba Illi River.

When he completed his missionary training Musa asked the Evangelical Church of Chad to appoint him as their missionary to the Mbororo people.

A Canadian, Vivian, travelled with us as far as Ba Illi where she was to work for a time. She had recently nursed in a clinic further north, where children would sometimes pelt her with stones as she walked to her work, while their elders looked away. She could not be sure if the community resented her as a foreigner or as a Christian. Even so, she hoped to return ultimately to serve her tormentors.

Another five hours driving on a badly rutted road brought us to the little town of Kouno. A nurse, this time from Scotland, welcomed us to her home. When I had last seen Joan MacKenzie she had been learning French. Now I heard her using Arabic as well as French. Following AIM policy in Chad, designed to foster flexibility in assignments, she rented a simple house belonging to a local landlord, who actually lived next door. I slept in the home of a couple who had recently departed for a few months in Britain, leaving Joan without other missionaries – an unusual situation for a single AIMer in Chad. I enquired, 'Where are the nearest people who speak English as their first language?' After a pause, she replied, 'Perhaps a hundred kilometres away.' But she never complained of loneliness. Her best friend, the landlord's daughter, came over to greet us from her home in the next dusty compound. And Joan told me she spent much time walking around the town, chatting to people. 'I sometimes wonder what my friends at home think', she said. 'Can they understand the importance of simply visiting homes and drinking tea in order to build relationships?'

Joan faced other misunderstandings closer to hand. She introduced me to Pastor Daniel who led a congregation in Kouno consisting of immigrants from the well-churched south. I had heard of these migrations and hoped they would result in a witness to the many tribes among whom the incomers settled. But I soon discovered that the immigrant church wished to enlarge their own tribal community, and did not share Joan's vision for helping all the tribes and especially those who knew nothing of the gospel. While rejoicing in fellowship with the Pastor and his little church, Joan agreed with another member of our team who told me, 'Perhaps our greatest challenge is to encourage the local churches to recognise their missionary responsibility to the Muslim tribes on their doorstep.'

But the health care work posed the greatest frustrations to Joan. Dr Marcus had rightly encouraged the Chadian Infirmier to lead the work. But how should a highly-qualified nurse from overseas relate to him? He stressed curative care while she focused on community health; he wanted her help in the clinic while she wished to work in the villages. To build relationships she agreed to assist the dispensary work part-time, though he treated her as a junior assistant. In return he consented to her taking a small team to vaccinate people in the villages and to train women in ante-natal care.

Joan, entertaining no starry-eyed expectations of quick results, took comfort in the certainty of Psalm 126:7:

'He who goes out weeping, carrying seed to sow, will return with songs of joy, carrying sheaves with him.'

*****

Our team had invited me to Chad to speak at their annual conference in N'djamena. Back in the city I learnt I could never take anything for granted. John had told me he could borrow a video player and asked if I could bring some films as a treat for his three boys as well as for the missionaries? They enjoyed the treat until the screen suddenly blanked out due to a power failure.

The city water supply was as unpredictable as electricity. I soon learnt that, at the first trickle of the precious fluid through the pipes, I must abandon all other activities and take a shower for I might have no further opportunity for hours, or even days.

Over five days we discussed together the amazing relevance of the ancient book of Daniel to modern Chad.

The Evangelical Alliance Mission also welcomed me to their missionary conference at a centre on the banks of the Chari, an hour's journey from N'djamena. In a bold recognition of the enormous task of evangelism still confronting them after sixty years of ministry in the south-west, they discussed the possibility of shifting their main focus from the established churches to the unreached. Should they ask the EET to release them for this new thrust? If so, when?

They all knew that those who enter unreached peoples will always face intense spiritual opposition. Two families, recently established in the northern desert, had set out on their 1,700 kilometre journey to join the conference. A zealous army officer arrested them on suspicion of spying. For nine days he and his soldiers travelled with them down to the city so that they could be further questioned. In the tense uncertainty one of the families found comfort in reciting Psalm 91 which the children had recently learnt. Tosha, one of the young mothers, praised God for the experience, 'It taught me that God loves us; his arms are always holding us tight; his peoples' prayers enfold us.' She would need that assurance to withstand the next blow.

Phanuel, a Christian soldier from the south, served in the north close to these families, joining them and a few others in worship on Sundays. Learning the local language, he began to share his faith with the tribes-people around him as well as taking a lead in the church. When he talked about resigning from the army and training for the ministry in order that he could return to pastor this little church, his fellow believers encouraged him. I had met him at Ba Illi, returning from the river with several fish skewered on a stick for his young wife to cook. He had already completed a year of seminary training in N'djamena and now was well into the missionary course. Two weeks later, while we met in conference, he became ill at Ba Illi. Paul, the Infirmier, treated him for malaria and he improved. But after two days he developed fits and Paul contacted John on the radio. John diagnosed tetanus and insisted that he come immediately to the city. Vivian drove him. Close to their destination they paused to adjust his saline drip. He recovered consciousness and said, 'It's all right. I've been in a beautiful place. Please take me to my uncle's home.' Five minutes after reaching his uncle, he died.

At the conference the news devastated us, particularly his fellow missionaries who had such high hopes for his future work. Questions seethed through my mind: when dark forces of evil were assaulting a promising work, why should the

Lord permit such loss? Where was the God of Daniel who had worked so powerfully for his people in the face of unjust political accusations and demonic assault? Then I recalled the three friends of Daniel who entered the fiery furnace telling the king, 'The God we serve is able to save us from it, and he will rescue us from your hand.' Then they added, 'But even if he does not we will not serve your gods or worship the image of gold you have set up.' God can be glorified in the death of his saints as much as in their deliverance; when the fire consumes them as well as when they walk free.

We prayed for Phanuel's young widow and their two children; then we sang,

For all the saints who from their labours rest,
Who thee by faith before the world confessed,
Thy Name, O Jesus, be for ever blest.
Alleluia! Alleluia.

On my way from the meeting I passed one of the ladies with an arm round Tosha as she wept, and my heart grieved. I thought of all the vigorous young churches across Africa, of the many still unreached people groups and I could hear Paul speaking for all gospel pioneers when he wrote, 'Death is at work in us but life in you' (2 Cor. 4:12).

16

POSTSCRIPT: PERISCOPIC PRAYER

I flew over a flooded area of South Sudan. Water spread for miles over black sticky soil, which would spell death to the unwary traveller who slipped in. A network of well-beaten paths also shone through the water and I realised there was a safe way through the morass, visible only from above. God's will for our lives, ministries and families is like a map known only to him. On the ground we may encounter perplexity and danger, but he knows the way through. He sees each turn of the track and, if we but cling to him, he will hold our hands until we emerge on the far side.

By 1990 Joan and I had served in the International Office for fifteen years – twelve of them in my capacity as IGS. The Mission wisely rules that a dozen years in this position is the maximum, so we bought our first house in a Scottish village with easy access to Mary and her family in Edinburgh. The IC asked us to continue speaking and writing on their behalf and the South African Council invited us to teach in three seminaries in Cape Town for eight happy months. We also visited Korea and Brazil several times to encourage recruits for Africa.

Seven years after leaving the office we retired. Unexpectedly this turn in our path proved one of the most radical. From a position of influence and responsibility, our decisions suddenly counted for very little. After years of almost constant movement we found ourselves static. Had

God terminated our ministry? Some said, 'You've earned your rest; take it easy.'

God's hand led us onwards over paths, familiar to many but new to us. He seemed to say, 'You can be as effective as ever right where you are', and he showed us afresh the immense power of prayer. We found more time both for personal intercession for unreached people throughout the world and for God's people who seek them and then serve the new young churches. Our village church in Scotland embraced us warmly and invited us to help in ministry. Joan and I could also give to our three close families the time we felt we often denied them in the past.

We now depend on others to keep us abreast with the needs of the world. By letters, e-mails and reports they kindly invite us to peep through their periscopes and what we see adds fuel to the fire burning in our bones.

Christian Focus Publications publishes biblically-accurate books for adults and children. The books in the adult range are published in three imprints.

Christian Heritage contains classic writings from the past.

Christian Focus contains popular works including biographies, commentaries, doctrine, and Christian living.

Mentor focuses on books written at a level suitable for Bible College and seminary students, pastors, and others; the imprint includes commentaries, doctrinal studies, examination of current issues, and church history.

For a free catalogue of all our titles, please write to
Christian Focus Publications,
Geanies House, Fearn,
Ross-shire, IV20 1TW, Great Britain

For details of our titles visit us on our web site
http://www.christianfocus.com